THE COMPLETE WORKS OF
CHRISTOPHER MARLOWE

Despite the modern fascination with Marlowe, there has been no edition of his works which not only gives them in the original spelling—with full textual apparatus—but also provides a detailed commentary. The Oxford English Texts *Complete Works of Christopher Marlowe* supplies the need for a fully annotated scholarly treatment of the works.

The present volume contains *The Jew of Malta*, one of the most imaginative creations of Elizabethan drama, having apparently no known sources or antecedents for the main events of its plot, and no counterpart—in life or in literature—for its protagonist. The introduction emphasizes the political importance of the Mediterranean island of Malta in the sixteenth century, suggesting that this could have been the dramatist's starting-point, and that Marlowe's experiences as petty spy and go-between somehow equipped him with the insight he needed to create his own world in *The Jew of Malta*.

ROMA GILL is a freelance writer and lecturer; her previous editions include *The Plays of Christopher Marlowe* (Oxford, 1971) and thirteen texts in the Oxford School Shakespeare Series. She was formerly a General Editor of the New Mermaid Texts (for which she edited three plays), and Reader in English Literature at the University of Sheffield.

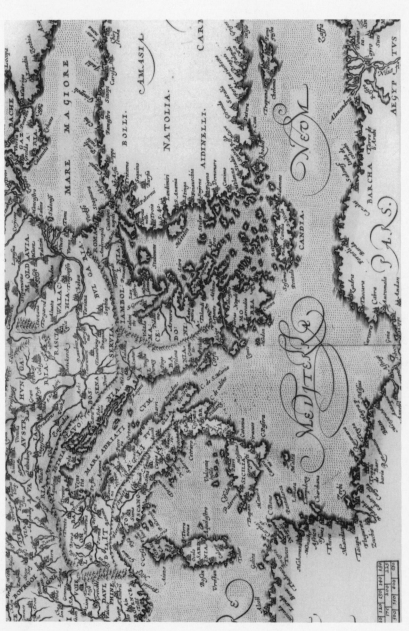

Map of the Mediterranean from Abraham Ortelius, Map 2 (Europa), *Theatrum Orbis Terrarum* (Antwerp, 1584).

THE COMPLETE WORKS
OF
CHRISTOPHER
MARLOWE

EDITED BY
ROMA GILL

VOLUME IV
The Jew of Malta

CLARENDON PRESS · OXFORD
1995

Oxford University Press, Walton Street, Oxford OX2 6DP

Oxford New York
Athens Auckland Bangkok Bombay
Calcutta Cape Town Dar es Salaam Delhi
Florence Hong Kong Istanbul Karachi
Kuala Lumpur Madras Madrid Melbourne
Mexico City Nairobi Paris Singapore
Taipei Tokyo Toronto
and associated companies in
Berlin Ibadan

Oxford is a trade mark of Oxford University Press

Published in the United States
by Oxford University Press, Inc. New York

British Library Cataloguing in Publication Data
Data available

Library of Congress Cataloging in Publication Data
Data available
ISBN 0-19-812770-7

1 3 5 7 9 10 8 6 4 2

Typeset by Hope Services (Abingdon) Ltd.
Printed in Great Britain
on acid-free paper by
Biddles Ltd.,
Guildford and King's Lynn

ACKNOWLEDGEMENTS

My thanks are due to the University of Sheffield for a travel grant awarded in 1970 so that I could visit the island and try to find some sort of answer to the overwhelming question, 'Why *Malta?*' And I am grateful to Brenda and the late James Packman for their friendship and hospitality on that and many subsequent visits to Malta. Every editor is bound to pay humble homage to predecessors, and I recognize my great indebtedness to the scholarship of N. W. Bawcutt's Revels edition of *The Jew of Malta*. Professor T. W. Craik gave freely of his wisdom and experience; my copy-editor, Leofranc Holford-Strevens, was generous with his erudition; Peter Fisher was indefatigable in tracking down references in the Cambridge University Library; and Cyril Hartley was patient, good-humoured, and entertaining whilst we laboured through 'Accidental Emendations'. Proofs of this text would never have been corrected without the unsparing efforts of Professor Craik and the willing assistance of Robert Lindsey. The British Academy afforded generous assistance for typing and other expenses. I thank them all.

R.G.

CONTENTS

Illustrations

INTRODUCTION

Marlowe and Malta

MARLOWE'S *Jew of Malta* must surely be reckoned one of the most imaginative creations of Elizabethan drama. There are no known sources or antecedents for the main events of its plot, and no counterpart—in life or in literature—for its protagonist! The play has defeated twentieth-century attempts to classify it: T. S. Eliot, noting the 'terribly serious, even savage comic humour', pronounced it a 'farce';[1] and Clifford Leech asked whether it should be called 'Black Comedy or Comic Tragedy'.[2] Perhaps it belongs in the genre described by Polonius (*Hamlet*, II. ii. 295) as 'tragical-comical-historical-pastoral'—with the addition 'satirical-topical'. And 'problematical'!

When I first started to edit *The Jew of Malta*, in 1970,[3] I found it a strangely unsettling experience. There were no major textual problems to speak of—after all, I had just confronted those of *Dr Faustus*! 'Black comedy' or 'tragic farce'? A Morality Play (*radix malorum cupiditas*)? An acting-out of the 'lecture' that Machevil (Prologue, l. 29) declines to read? These were all fruitful avenues (and some of them were well-trodden ways) for exploration—but for me they all proved dead ends, leaving me still with the same uneasiness, which eventually formulated itself into the question WHY—why *Malta*? Marlowe's play has no starting-point—it comes from nowhere. *Dido* springs out of the *Aeneid*, *Tamburlaine* is framed out of the many stories of Timur the Lame, *Edward II* is rooted in Holinshed's *Chronicles*, and *Dr Faustus* translates readily from the Wittenberg of *The English Faustbook* to the Cambridge of Marlowe's youth. But where did *The Jew* come from? What was the peculiar spark that lighted Marlowe's fire?

In desperation I took a holiday—and went to Malta.

Marlowe seems to have known a lot about the island of

---

[1] 'Christopher Marlowe', in T. S. Eliot, *Selected Essays* (London: Faber and Faber, 1932; 3rd edn. 1951), 123; repr. in Clifford Leech (ed.), *Marlowe: A Collection of Critical Essays* (Englewood Cliffs, NJ: Prentice-Hall Inc., 1964), 16.

[2] *Christopher Marlowe: Poet for the Stage* (New York: AMS Press, 1986), 159.

[3] For *The Plays of Christopher Marlowe* (London: Oxford University Press, 1971).

Malta, its geography, and its recent history. In the play's first scene Barabas, its protagonist, defines Malta's precise location. Looking out from his counting-house, he can see the weather-vanes and his 'Halcions bill', which are indicating a wind direction 'East and by-South'. From this quarter the wind will bring his 'Argosie from *Alexandria*' safely 'through our *Mediterranean* sea', passing the island of Crete ('by *Candie* shoare'), to harbour in '*Malta* Rhode' (ll. 49 ff.). When he interviews the merchant-seamen, Barabas demonstrates his knowledge of sea-lanes. He is surprised that the captain of the 'Speranza' has not seen the missing argosy, telling him

> Thou couldst not come from *Egypt*, or by *Caire*
> But at the entry there into the sea,
> Where *Nilus* payes his tribute to the maine,
> Thou needs must saile by *Alexandria*. (71–4).

The captain of the missing ship soon appears, however, although he can offer no explanation for his failure to rendezvous with the main body of the fleet. But Barabas knows about the traffic in these lanes, and suggests that they had probably 'coasted round by *Candie* shoare About their Oyles, or other businesses' (ll. 89–90). Barabas also knows that these are dangerous waters, and he reprimands the captain for his foolhardiness in attempting the voyage without escort. There is an explanation however—the solitary vessel had been protected by a Spanish fleet 'That had the Gallies of the Turke in chase'. Again Barabas understands: 'they were going up to *Sicily*'.

Most of this information was available in Marlowe's favourite atlas, the *Theatrum Orbis Terrarum* of Ortelius, which he had used to map the travels and conquests of Tamburlaine.[4] But Malta is a tiny island—at its longest and widest points it measures no more than eighteen miles by nine miles—and it shows as only a speck in Ortelius's Mediterranean. Marlowe must have had access to some other source for what he knows of the island's topography. The earliest of all known maps of Malta was drawn by a French knight, Jean Quintin.[5] Its scope includes the 'other petty Iles'—Gozo, Comino, Cominotto, and Filfla—with

[4] See M. E. Seaton, 'Marlowe's Map', *Essays and Studies*, 10 (1924), 13–35.

[5] Printed in Quintin's *Insulae Melitae Descriptio ex Commentariis Rerum Quotidianarum* (Lyons: Seb. Gryphius, 1536) f.A2ᵛ; the original is in the Museum and Library of the Order of St John, in Clerkenwell, London.

which Malta is 'contermur'd' (v. iii. 9), and it set the example
for other sixteenth-century cartographers, who all give the same
information (making it impossible to identify any one particular
map as the one that Marlowe *must* have used). They all outline
creeks and name villages and, in the position of the ancient capi-
tal Mdina, they mark a central, often towered, 'Civitas' or
'Oppidum'. Marlowe's characters similarly have no particular
name for their local habitation, and they refer generally to the
'Towne'—which appears to combine the facilities of the walled
city of Mdina and the fortified township Birgu (in Act V Scene i
Barabas, feigning death, is thrown over city walls—only to arise,
three lines later, in a position to greet the invading Calymath).
Near the biggest of the harbours Quintin's map indicates, using
cartographer's turrets, the twin forts of St Elmo and St Angelo
(identified as 'C. Santangelo'). For the purposes of the play,
these became the 'Two lofty Turrets that command the Towne'
(v. iii. 3) which are destroyed by the Turks under their leader,
Selim Calymath, in the play's imagined siege.

The Great Siege of Malta is a historical fact, and Selim
Calymath, the son of Süleyman the Magnificent, was a real-life
person. But the play bears little resemblance to what actually
happened. There was never any tributary league of the sort that
horrifies Del Bosco in Act II Scene ii: 'Will Knights of *Malta* be
in league with Turkes, And buy it basely too for summes of
gold?' (ll. 28–9). The Turks coveted Malta and the other
Mediterranean islands for their many creeks and harbours, which
would afford shelter to the fighting-ships protecting the Holy
Land against the Christian crusaders—and which might be used
for launching an attack on the 'soft underbelly' of Europe. They
besieged Malta in 1565, and there was fierce fighting around the
fort of St Elmo. But the Turks were defeated, and the island
was never captured. Mediterranean history of the sixteenth century is rich in accounts of Turkish sieges and stratagems; there
are even stories of a rich Jew, Joseph Nasi, who was made duke
of Naxos for services rendered to the Turks. The subject has
been well researched in the hunt for sources for *The Jew of
Malta*, and a few analogues have been found,[6] but ultimately
these can only confirm the originality of Marlowe's invention.

[6] See *The Jew of Malta*, ed. N. W. Bawcutt (The Revels Plays: Manchester
University Press, 1978), 4–16.

At the beginning of the sixteenth century Malta was a Spanish possession, and in 1530 Charles V of Spain presented the island to the Knights Hospitallers, of St John, after the Turks had driven them out of Rhodes. In the play, Martin del Bosco reminds Ferneze and his Knights of this fact:

> Remember that to *Europ's* shame
> The Christian Ile of *Rhodes*, from whence you came,
> Was lately lost, and you were stated here
> To be at deadly enmity with Turkes.   (II. ii. 30–3.)

Ferneze's function seems to be that of the Grand Master of the Order, although the character has an additional social dimension as the father of Lodowicke. In their original foundation, the Knights Hospitallers were defenders of the faith and protectors of Christian pilgrims on their journeys to Jerusalem. They gained some heroic stature after the siege of Rhodes, and the whole of England prayed for them when the Turks attacked Malta in 1565.[7] Apart from this, however, the Order was not popular. Its members were drawn from the aristocracy of every nation in Europe, and owed direct allegiance to none but the Pope; they were rich, and lived by what Ernle Bradford called 'organized piracy'.[8] They freed the Christian slaves who rowed the Turkish galleys—and chained their own prisoners to the oars with equal brutality. Gibbon said that 'They neglected to live, but were prepared to die, in the service of Christ.'[9] Marlowe's Knights are odious—but not incredibly so. To raise money for the unpaid tribute to the Turks, they impose a levy on the Jews with the threat of enforced baptism for those who refuse to pay:

---

[7] In England the bishops ordained diocesan prayers, issuing 'A Fourme | to be used in Common | prayer every Wednesdaye and | Frydaye, within the Cittie | and Dioces of London: | to excite all godly peo|ple to praye un|to God for the | delivery | of those Christians, that | are now invaded by | the Turke'; title-page reproduced in Andrew P. Vella, *An Elizabethan–Ottoman Conspiracy* (Mnida: University of Malta Press, 1972), 14.

[8] Ernle Bradford, *The Great Siege: Malta 1565* (London: Hodder & Stoughton, 1961), 21. For a more favourable view of the Order see H. J. A. Sire, *The Knights of Malta* (New Haven and London: Yale University Press, 1994); on the siege see pp. 68–72.

[9] *The Decline and Fall of the Roman Empire*, ed. J. B. Bury, 7 vols. (London: Methuen, 1909–14), vi. 329 (ch. 58).

First, the tribute mony of the Turkes shall all be levyed amongst the
Jewes, and each of them to pay one halfe of his estate . . . Secondly,
hee that denies to pay, shal straight become a Christian. (I. ii.
68–74.)

By any modern standards this is outrageous; but the historical truth is not very different. In 1492, before the arrival of the
Knights of St John, the ruling class in Malta (who came from
old Sicilian and Castilian families) expelled all Jews from the
island—except for those individuals who agreed to purchase
Christian baptism at the price of 45 per cent of their total
wealth. Twentieth-century ears are shocked by the unctuous-
ness of the Knight's rejoinder to Barabas:

> If your first curse fall heavy on thy head
> And make thee poore and scorn'd of all the world,
> 'Tis not our fault, but thy inherent sinne.

> (I. ii. 108–10.)

Yet he articulates no more than many Elizabethan Christians
would believe.

In his opposition to the Knights Barabas, their victim, is
almost heroic. At the beginning of the play his self-revelatory
soliloquies and conspiratorial 'asides' enlist the spectators' sympathy in much the same way as do those of a contemporary
grotesque, Shakespeare's Richard III. Marlowe has thoroughly
researched a Jewish identity for Barabas, creating from the Old
Testament a character far richer than any of the stereotypes that
he could have inherited from popular tradition (which would
only have given him the features that Ithimore can describe).
Against his Christian persecutors, Barabas proudly maintains his
own identity as a Jew, a member of God's chosen race ('unto us
the Promise doth belong', II. iii. 48). But privately he cares little
for the nationality: 'They say we are a scatter'd Nation: I cannot
tell' (I. i. 118–19). The other Jews flock to him, as to their
leader, in time of crisis: 'let us goe to *Barrabas*; For he can counsell best in these affaires' (I. i. 138–9); but their leader deserts
them in the same breath as he promises aid: 'Assure your selves
I'le looke unto (*aside*) my selfe' (l. 170). When Barabas himself
is in distress, the other three Jews, ignorant of his treachery,
cast themselves into the role of the Job's comforters—but
Barabas disdains to accept the part they design for him:

What tell you me of *Job*? . . .
I had at home, and in mine *Argosie*
And other ships that came from *Egypt* last,
As much as would have bought his beasts and him.

(i. ii. 181–9.)

Barabas is Marlowe's own multi-faceted creation; his individuality encompasses the careful tradesman who counts his 'paltry silverlings', the near-visionary who would accumulate 'Infinite riches in a little roome', and the father who loves his daughter 'As *Agamemnon* did his *Iphigen*'—qualifying his love even as he boasts it. The revenge plot develops from the character thus elemented in the first act of the play. As the plot gathers pace, the character dwindles—and audience sympathy recedes.

No other character engages our feelings for very long. The innocent Abigall has a momentary pathos in her death, but this is immediately dissolved in a crude joke:

ABIGALL. Convert my father that he may be sav'd,
And witnesse that I dye a Christian.
2 FRYAR. I, and a Virgin too, that grieves me most.

(III. vi. 39–41.)

The remaining characters are stereotypes, more or less caricatured: the Friars are lustful and avaricious (although they acknowledge the secrecy of the confessional, III. vi. 33–6); Abigall's lovers are easily enamoured and easily duped; the mother who laments the death of Don Mathias is no more than a 'Mater'—even her name (she is 'Katherin' in III. ii. 16) seems to have been an afterthought. But what is remarkable is their heterogeneity—Turks and Jews; Christian Knights, friars, and nuns; aristocrats and the low-life confraternity of slave, pimp, and prostitute.

In the sixteenth century there was only one place on earth—Malta—that would have given entertainment to such a contradiction of characters. How much did Marlowe know about the island, and where did he get his information from? He could have read Malta's history in books—there were several in French, Italian, and Spanish, although little was written in English; and he might have acquired an appreciation of the island's geography through his skill as a map-reader. But books

and maps alone cannot explain his interest. Marlowe seems to
be strangely sensitive to the peculiar political and religious ten-
sions of contemporary Malta, and such sensitivity is unlikely to
have been learned from literature. I would suggest that
Marlowe's experiences as petty spy and go-between somehow
equipped him with the insight he needed to create his own
world in *The Jew of Malta*.

The establishment of the Levant Trading Company in 1581
forced an uneasy but economic alliance between the English
and their traditional enemies, the Turks. A new enemy,
Catholic Spain, was threatening the Protestant monarchy, and
to counter this the English were developing their espionage
network in the Mediterranean. Much more research is needed
on this subject, but one—albeit trivial—incident has been
brought to light by Professor Andrew Vella, late Professor of
History in the University of Malta. In his book *An
Elizabethan–Ottoman Conspiracy* he describes how an English
ship, the *Roe*, landed in Malta in 1581. Captain and crew were
apprehended and subjected to inquisition by one Monsignor
Cefalotto, who reported the incident to his superiors in Rome
with the warning:

It is a well-known fact that the friendship between the English and
the Prince of this island [La Cassiere] and the ambitions and desires
of the Knights would impel them to do all kind of harm to the
Catholic Commonwealth and to the King of Spain. For this purpose
there cannot be an easier place from where to assault and cause havoc
than from Malta, because of its strategic position . . .[10]

Marlowe's acquaintance was wider and more varied than his
career as dramatist would suggest. There are ever fresh details
coming to light about the murky underworld which he inhab-
ited and the shabby individuals with whom he conversed—
those who secured his degree in 1586, those who occasioned his
presence in Flushing in 1592, and the ones who seem to have
engineered his death in Deptford in 1593.[11] Among these, perhaps, are some whose names and activities would throw light
on *The Jew of Malta*.

---

[10] Tr. Vella, 56.
[11] See e.g. Charles Nicholl, *The Reckoning* (London: Jonathan Cape, 1992).

Date and Text

ON 26 February 1592 Henslowe recorded the receipt of fifty shillings a performance by the Lord Strange's Men of 'the Jewe of malltuse'; and his *Diary* entry[12] provides a definite *terminus ad quem* for Marlowe's play. This may well not have been the first performance, since the play is not marked 'ne(w)'. The *terminus a quo* would seem to be supplied by a reference in the Machevil Prologue, 'now the *Guize* is dead'; the Duke of Guise was assassinated by Henri III's command on 23 December 1588.

Frequent performances—there were seventeen in the twelve months between 1592 and 1593—no doubt earned the play its description as *the famous tragedie of the Riche Jew of Malta* when it was entered for Nicholas Ling and Thomas Millington in the Stationers' Register on 17 May 1594. Apparently no publication resulted from this entry. The play was entered again on 20 November 1632, when it was licensed by Sir Henry Herbert to be published by Nicholas Vavasour. The following year it was printed by John Beale (STC 17412):

The Famous | TRAGEDY | OF | THE RICH IEW | OF *MALTA*. | AS IT WAS PLAYD | BEFORE THE KING AND | QUEENE, IN HIS MAJESTIES | Theatre at *White-Hall*, by her Majesties | Servants at the *Cock-pit*. | *Written by* CHRISTOPHER MARLO. | [type ornament] | LONDON; | Printed by *I.B.* for *Nicholas Vavasour*, and are to be sold | at his Shop in the Inner-Temple, neere the | Church. 1633. 4° A–I⁴, K²; A1, 2 blank; A3 Epistle by THO. HEYWOOD.; A4ʳ The Prologue spoken at Court, Epilogue; A4ᵛ The Prologue to the Stage, at the Cocke-pit, Epilogue; B1ʳ text starts; K2ᵛ text ends FINIS.

Bawcutt describes the 1633 quarto as 'a very ordinary piece of book production': the worn type is imperfectly inked, literals abound, prose is frequentedly printed as verse, speech-prefixes are irregular, and 'asides' are erratically indicated. Circumstances have compelled me to rely on the collations of other editors; but only the most minimal press-correction was detected by Bawcutt (who collated 14 copies) and Bowers (12 copies). Both editors incline to the view that MS underlying Q is some kind of transcript, perhaps Marlowe's fair copy of his

---

[12] Philip Henslowe, *Diary*, ed. R. A. Foakes and R. T. Rickert (Cambridge University Press, 1961), 16.

foul papers (Bawcutt), or else (Bowers) a transcript of the the-
atrical promptbook. Craik argues for a playhouse manuscript,
attributing the many confusions in the spelling of proper names
to the printer's having expanded the abbreviations which he
found in his copy. The frequent mislineation, and the unintelli-
gible Spanish in Act I Scene ii, are similarly accounted for.
Recent evidence presented by Dr D. J. Lake supports this
view.[13] Basing his argument on colloquial contractions ('*em* for
'them', *i'th* and *o'th*), Lake identifies the style of Thomas
Dekker, and suggests that Dekker may have introduced some of
his own mannerisms into the play whilst copying the text at the
beginning of the seventeenth century. For this edition I have
used the photographs in The Scolar Press reprint (Menston,
1970) of the Bodleian copy Mal. 172(2), occasionally checked
against the far clearer copy Mal. 915(5). Unless misleadingly
erroneous, the original spelling and punctuation are retained—
although the usages of *i/j*, *u/v* have been normalized. Evident
mislining of verse and prose has been corrected and noted in
'Emendation of Accidentals', along with the printer's errors in
the attribution of speeches. Proper names have been uniformly
italicized. All asides are marked as such, square brackets indicating any variation from Q's erratic practice; I have not, however, followed Q in its occasional use of italics for the words to
be thus spoken. Additional stage directions are enclosed in
square brackets. In the matter of speech prefixes I have been
guided by Craik, who recognized that some characters are
named typically rather than individually ('Governor', 'Mater',
'Curtezane' rather than 'Ferneze', 'Katherin', and 'Bellamira'),
and that this 'throws into proper relief' the naming of more
distinguished characters (Barabas, Ithimore, Calymath, and Del
Bosco). Q's speech prefixes are usually abbreviated; here the
full names (titles or descriptions) are given, in accordance with
those listed in the *Dramatis Personae*.

---

[13] 'Three Seventeenth-Century Revisions: *Thomas of Woodstock*, *The Jew of Malta*,
and *Faustus B*', *Notes & Queries*, NS 30/2 (Apr. 1983), 133–43.

Map of Malta from Jean Quintin d'Autun, *Insulae Melitae Descriptio ex Commentariis Rerum Quotidianarum* (Lyons: Seb. Gryphius, 1536).

REFERENCES AND ABBREVIATIONS

Editions of The Jew of Malta

1. *Single Texts*

Q *The Famous Tragedy of the Rich Jew of Malta* (London: Nicholas Vavasour, 1633).

Bawcutt *The Jew of Malta*, ed. N. W. Bawcutt (Manchester University Press; Baltimore: Johns Hopkins University Press, 1978).

Broughton *The Famous Tragedy of the Rich Jew of Malta*, ed. James Broughton (London: J. Chappell Jr, 1818).

Craik *The Jew of Malta*, ed. T. W. Craik (London: Ernest Benn Ltd, 1966).

Penley *Marlowe's Celebrated Tragedy of the Jew of Malta . . . With Considerable Alterations and Additions.* By S. Penley, Comedian (London: Richard White, 1818).

Reed *A Select Collection of Old Plays*, ed. Robert Dodsley, 2nd edn. ed. Isaac Reed (London: J. Dodsley, 1780), VIII.

Scott *The Ancient British Drama*, ed. Sir Walter Scott, (London: William Miller, 1810), i.

Shone *The Famous Historical Tragedy of the Rich Jew of Malta . . . Imitated from the Works of Machiavelli, by Christopher Marlo*, ? ed. W. Shone (London: Reynell and Son, 1810).

2. *Complete Editions*

Bennett *The Jew of Malta* and *The Massacre at Paris*, ed. H. S. Bennett, in *The Works and Life of Christopher Marlowe*, ed. R. H. Case (London: Methuen, 1930–3), iii (1931).

Bowers *The Complete Works of Christopher Marlowe*, ed. Fredson Bowers (2 vols., Cambridge University Press, 1973), i.

Bullen *The Works of Christopher Marlowe*, ed. A. H. Bullen (London: John C. Nimmo, 1885).

Collier *A Select Collection of Old Plays*: A New Edition, ed. J. P. Collier (London: Septimus Prowett, 1825), VIII.

Dyce *The Works of Christopher Marlowe with Notes and Some Account of his life and writings by the Rev. Alexander Dyce* (London: William Pickering, 1850).

Robinson   *The Works of Christopher Marlowe*, ed. G. Robinson
(London: William Pickering, 1826).

Quotations

Quotations from Marlowe's other works are taken from *The Complete
Works of Christopher Marlowe*, vol. i, *Translations*, and vol. ii, *Dr
Faustus*, ed. Roma Gill (Oxford University Press, 1987 and 1990); and
from Bowers.

Hunter   G. K. Hunter, 'The Theology of Marlowe's *The Jew of
Malta*', *Journal of the Warburg and Courtauld Institutes*,
27 (1964), 211-40; repr. in id., *Dramatic Identities and
Cultural Tradition: Studies in Shakespeare and his
Contemporaries* (Liverpool: University Press, 1978),
60-102.

Bible   *The Bible and Holy Scriptures Conteyned in the Olde and
Newe Testament* (Geneva: Rouland Hall, 1560).

Shakespeare   The Riverside Edition, ed. G. Blakemore Evans *et al.*
(Boston: Houghton Mifflin, 1974).

Other Abbreviations

OED   *The Oxford English Dictionary.*
om.   *omitted.*
SD   stage direction.
Tilley   M. P. Tilley, *A Dictionary of the Proverbs in England in the
Sixteenth and Seventeenth Centuries* (Ann Arbor: University of
Michigan Press, 1950).

TRAGEDY

OF

THE RICH IEVV

OF MALTA.

AS IT VVAS PLAYD
BEFORE THE KING AND
QVEENE, IN HIS MAJESTIES
Theatre at *White-Hall*, by her Majesties
Servants at the *Cock-pit*.

Written by CHRISTOPHER MARLO.

LONDON;
Printed by *I. B.* for *Nicholas Vavasour*, and are to be sold
at his Shop in the Inner-Temple, neere the
Church. 1633.

[Dramatis Personae

MACHEVIL	*Prologue*
BARABAS	*the Jew of Malta*
ABIGALL	*the Jew's daughter*
ITHIMORE	*the Jew's slave*
GOVERNOR	*of Malta*
DON LODOWICK	*the Governor's son*
DON MATHIAS	*friend to Don Lodowick*
MATER	*mother of Mathias*
SELIM CALYMATH	*son to the Grand Signior of Turkey*
BASSO	*to Calymath*
MARTIN DEL BOSCO	*the Spanish Vice-Admiral*
1 FRYAR (Jacomo)	
2 FRYAR (Bernardine)	
ABBASSE	
PILIA-BORZA	
CURTEZANE	
Two MERCHANTS	
Three JEWS	

Knights, Bassoes, Officers, Nun, Slaves, Messenger, Carpenters.]

The
Jew of
Malta

[*Prologue.*]

[*Enter*] MACHEVIL.

Albeit the world thinke *Machevill* is dead,
Yet was his soule but flowne beyond the *Alpes*,
And now the *Guize* is dead, is come from *France*
To view this Land, and frolicke with his friends.
To some perhaps my name is odious,   5
But such as love me, gard me from their tongues,
And let them know that I am *Machevill*,
And weigh not men, and therefore not mens words:
Admir'd I am of those that hate me most.
Though some speake openly against my bookes,   10
Yet will they reade me, and thereby attaine
To *Peters* Chayre: And when they cast me off,
Are poyson'd by my climing followers.
I count Religion but a childish Toy,
And hold there is no sinne but Ignorance.   15
Birds of the Aire will tell of murders past;
I am asham'd to heare such fooleries:
Many will talke of Title to a Crowne.
What right had *Caesar* to the Empery?
Might first made Kings, and Lawes were then most sure 20
When like the *Dracos* they were writ in blood.
Hence comes it, that a strong built Citadell
Commands much more then letters can import:
Which maxime had *Phaleris* observ'd,
H'had never bellowed in a brasen Bull   25
Of great ones envy; o'th poore petty wites,
Let me be envy'd and not pittied!
But whither am I bound, I come not, I,
To reade a lecture here in *Britanie*,
But to present the Tragedy of a Jew,   30

Who smiles to see how full his bags are cramb'd
Which mony was not got without my meanes.
I crave but this, Grace him as he deserves,
And let him not be entertain'd the worse
Because he favours me.   [*Exit.*] 35

Actus Primus [*Scaena 1*].

Enter BARABAS *in his Counting-house,*
with heapes of gold before him.

BARABAS. So that of thus much that returne was made:
And of the third part of the Persian ships,
There was the venture summ'd and satisfied.
As for those Samnites, and the men of *Uzz*,
That bought my Spanish Oyles, and Wines of *Greece*,   5
Here have I purst their paltry silverlings.
Fye; what a trouble tis to count this trash.
Well fare the Arabians, who so richly pay,
The things they traffique for with wedge of gold,
Whereof a man may easily in a day   10
Tell that which may maintaine him all his life.
The needy groome that never fingred groat,
Would make a miracle of thus much coyne:
But he whose steele-bard coffers are cramb'd full,
And all his life time hath bin tired,   15
Wearying his fingers ends with telling it,
Would in his age be loath to labour so,
And for a pound to sweat himselfe to death:
Give me the Merchants of the Indian Mynes,
That trade in mettall of the purest mould;   20
The wealthy Moore, that in the Easterne rockes
Without controule can picke his riches up,
And in his house heape pearle like pibble-stones,
Receive them free, and sell them by the weight;
Bags of fiery Opals, Saphires, Amatists,   25
Jacints, hard Topas, grasse-greene Emeraulds,
Beauteous Rubyes, sparkling Diamonds,
And seildsene costly stones of so great price,
As one of them indifferently rated,
And of a Carrect of this quantity,   30
May serve in perill of calamity
To ransome great Kings from captivity.
This is the ware wherein consists my wealth:
And thus me thinkes should men of judgement frame

Their meanes of traffique from the vulgar trade,   35
And as their wealth increaseth, so inclose
Infinite riches in a little roome.
But now how stands the wind?
Into what corner peeres my Halcions bill?
Ha, to the East? yes: See how stands the Vanes?   40
East and by-South: why then I hope my ships
I sent for *Egypt* and the bordering Iles
Are gotten up by *Nilus* winding bankes:
Mine Argosie from *Alexandria*,
Loaden with Spice and Silkes, now under saile,   45
Are smoothly gliding downe by *Candie* shoare
To *Malta*, through our *Mediterranean* sea.
But who comes heare?

Enter a MERCHANT.

How now.

1 MERCHANT.   *Barabas*,
Thy ships are safe, riding in *Malta* Rhode:
And all the Merchants with ther Merchandize   50
Are safe arriv'd, and have sent me to know
Whether your selfe will come and custome them.

BARABAS. The ships are safe thou saist, and richly fraught.

1 MERCHANT. They are.

BARABAS.   Why then goe bid them come ashore,
And bring with them their bils of entry: 55
I hope our credit in the Custome-house
Will serve as well as I were present there.
Goe send 'um threescore Camels, thirty Mules,
And twenty Waggons to bring up the ware.
But art thou master in a ship of mine,   60
And is thy credit not enough for that?

1 MERCHANT. The very Custome barely comes to more
Then many Merchants of the Towne are worth,
And therefore farre exceeds my credit, Sir.

BARABAS. Goe tell 'em the Jew of *Malta* sent thee, man: 65
Tush, who amongst 'em knowes not *Barrabas*?

1 MERCHANT. I goe.

50 ther] other *Q*

BARABAS.   So then, there's somewhat come.
   Sirra, which of my ships art thou Master of?
1 MERCHANT. Of the *Speranza*, Sir.
BARABAS.   And saw'st thou not
   Mine Argosie at *Alexandria*?   70
   Thou couldst not come from *Egypt*, or by *Caire*
   But at the entry there into the sea,
   Where *Nilus* payes his tribute to the maine,
   Thou needs must saile by *Alexandria*.
1 MERCHANT. I neither saw them, nor inquir'd of them.   75
   But this we heard some of our sea-men say,
   They wondred how you durst with so much wealth
   Trust such a crazed Vessell, and so farre.
BARABAS. Tush, they are wise; I know her and her strength:
   But goe, goe thou thy wayes, discharge thy Ship,   80
   And bid my Factor bring his loading in.
                                    [*Exit* 1 MERCHANT.]
   And yet I wonder at this Argosie.

                 Enter a second MERCHANT.

2 MERCHANT. Thine Argosie from *Alexandria*,
   Know *Barabas* doth ride in *Malta* Rhode,
   Laden with riches, and exceeding store   85
   Of Persian silkes, of gold, and Orient Perle:
BARABAS. How chance you came not with those other ships
   That sail'd by *Egypt*?
2 MERCHANT.   Sir we saw 'em not.
BARABAS. Belike they coasted round by *Candie* shoare
   About their Oyles, or other businesses.   90
   But 'twas ill done of you to come so farre
   Without the ayd or conduct of their ships.
2 MERCHANT. Sir, we were wafted by a Spanish Fleet
   That never left us till within a league,
   That had the Gallies of the Turke in chase.   95
BARABAS. Oh they were going up to *Sicily*: well, goe
   And bid the Merchants and my men dispatch
   And come ashore, and see the fraught discharg'd.
2 MERCHANT. I goe.   *Exit.*

       68 Master of] *Reed*; ~ off *Q*   80 But] *Shone*; By *Q*

BARABAS. Thus trowles our fortune in by land and Sea,   100
    And thus are wee on every side inrich'd:
    These are the Blessings promis'd to the Jewes,
    And herein was old *Abrams* happinesse:
    What more may Heaven doe for earthly men
    Then thus to powre out plenty in their laps,   105
    Ripping the bowels of the earth for them,
    Making the Seas their servants, and the winds
    To drive their substance with successefull blasts?
    Who hateth me but for my happinesse?
    Or who is honour'd now but for his wealth?   110
    Rather had I a Jew be hated thus,
    Then pittied in a Christian poverty:
    For I can see no fruits in all their faith,
    But malice, falshood, and excessive pride,
    Which me thinkes fits not their profession.   115
    Happily some haplesse man hath conscience,
    And for his conscience lives in beggery.
    They say we are a scatter'd Nation:
    I cannot tell, but we have scambled up
    More wealth by farre then those that brag of faith.   120
    There's *Kirriah Jairim*, the great Jew of *Greece*,
    Obed in *Bairseth*, *Nones* in *Portugall*,
    My selfe in *Malta*, some in *Italy*,
    Many in *France*, and wealthy every one:
    I, wealthier farre then any Christian.   125
    I must confesse we come not to be Kings:
    That's not our fault: Alas, our number's few,
    And Crownes come either by succession,
    Or urg'd by force; and nothing violent,
    Oft have I heard tell, can be permanent.   130
    Give us a peacefull rule, make Christians Kings,
    That thirst so much for Principality.
    I have no charge, nor many children,
    But one sole Daughter, whom I hold as deare
    As *Agamemnon* did his *Iphigen*:   135
    And all I have is hers. But who comes here?

Enter three JEWES.

104 men] *Shone*; man *Q*   107 Seas] *Broughton*; Sea *Q*

1 JEW. Tush, tell not me, 'twas done of policie.
2 JEW. Come therefore let us goe to *Barrabas*;
   For he can counsell best in these affaires;
   And here he comes.
BARABAS.   Why how now Countrymen?   140
   Why flocke you thus to me in multitudes?
   What accident's betided to the Jewes?
1 JEW. A Fleet of warlike Gallyes, *Barabas*,
   Are come from *Turkey*, and lye in our Rhode:
   And they this day sit in the Counsell-house   145
   To entertaine them and their Embassie.
BARABAS. Why let 'em come, so they come not to warre;
   Or let 'em warre, so we be conquerors:
   Nay, let 'em combat, conquer, and kill all,   *Aside.*
   So they spare me, my daughter, and my wealth.   150
1 JEW. Were it for confirmation of a League,
   They would not come in warlike manner thus.
2 JEW. I feare their comming will afflict us all.
BARABAS. Fond men, what dreame you of their multitudes?
   What need they treat of peace that are in league?   155
   The Turkes and those of *Malta* are in league.
   Tut, tut, there is some other matter in't.
1 JEW. Why, *Barabas*, they come for peace or warre.
BARABAS. Happily for neither, but to passe along
   Towards *Venice* by the *Adriatick* Sea;   160
   With whom they have attempted many times,
   But never could effect their Strategem.
3 JEW. And very wisely sayd, it may be so.
2 JEW. But there's a meeting in the Senate-house,
   And all the Jewes in *Malta* must be there.   165
BARABAS. Umh; all the Jewes in *Malta* must be there?
   I, like enough, why then let every man
   Provide him, and be there for fashion-sake.
   If any thing shall there concerne our state
   Assure your selves I'le looke unto (*aside*) my selfe. 170
1 JEW. I know you will; well brethren let us goe.
2 JEW. Let's take our leaves; Farewell good *Barabas*.
                                    [*Exeunt* JEWES.]
BARABAS. Doe so; Farewell *Zaareth*, farewell *Temanite*.
   And *Barabas* now search this secret out.

Summon thy sences, call thy wits together: 175
These silly men mistake the matter cleane.
Long to the Turke did *Malta* contribute;
Which Tribute all in policie, I feare,
The Turkes have let increase to such a summe,
As all the wealth of *Malta* cannot pay;   180
And now by that advantage thinkes, belike,
To seize upon the Towne: I, that he seekes.
How ere the world goe, I'le make sure for one,
And seeke in time to intercept the worst,
Warily garding that which I ha got.   185
Ego mihimet sum semper proximus.
Why let 'em enter, let 'em take the Towne.   [*Exit.*]

[*Scaena* 2.]

Enter GOVERNOR *of* Malta, KNIGHTS [*and* OFFICERS]
met by BASSOES *of the* Turke; CALYMATH.

GOVERNOR. Now Bassoes, what demand you at our hands?

BASSO. Know Knights of *Malta*, that we came from *Rhodes*,
From *Cyprus*, *Candy*, and those other Iles
That lye betwixt the *Mediterranean* seas.

GOVERNOR. What's *Cyprus*, *Candy*, and those other Iles   5
To us, or *Malta*? What at our hands demand ye?

CALYMATH. The ten yeares tribute that remaines unpaid.

GOVERNOR. Alas, my Lord, the summe is overgreat,
I hope your Highnesse will consider us.

CALYMATH. I wish, grave Governour 'twere in my power   10
To favour you, but 'tis my fathers cause,
Wherein I may not, nay I dare not dally.

GOVERNOR. Then give us leave, great *Selim-Calymath*.

CALYMATH. Stand all aside, and let the Knights determine,
And send to keepe our Gallies under-saile,   15
For happily we shall not tarry here:
Now Governour how are you resolv'd?

GOVERNOR. Thus: Since your hard conditions are such
That you will needs have ten yeares tribute past,
We may have time to make collection   20
Amongst the Inhabitants of *Malta* for't.

BASSO. That's more then is in our Commission.

CALYMATH. What *Callapine* a little curtesie.
Let's know their time, perhaps it is not long;
And 'tis more Kingly to obtaine by peace   25
Then to enforce conditions by constraint.
What respit aske you Governour?

GOVERNOR.   But a month.

CALYMATH. We grant a month, but see you keep your promise.
Now lanch our Gallies backe againe to Sea,
Where wee'll attend the respit you have tane,   30
And for the mony send our messenger.
Farewell great Governour, and brave Knights of *Malta*.
                                 Exeunt [Turkes].

GOVERNOR. And all good fortune wait on *Calymath*.
Goe one and call those Jewes of *Malta* hither:
Were they not summon'd to appeare to day?   35
OFFICER. They were, my Lord, and here they come.

Enter BARABAS, *and three* JEWES.

1 KNIGHT. Have you determin'd what to say to them?
GOVERNOR. Yes, give me leave, and Hebrews now come neare.
From the Emperour of *Turkey* is arriv'd
Great *Selim-Calymath*, his Highnesse sonne,   40
To levie of us ten yeares tribute past,
Now then, here know that it concerneth us:
BARABAS. Then, good my Lord, to keepe your quiet still,
Your Lordship shall doe well to let them have it.
GOVERNOR. Soft *Barabas*, there's more longs too't than so.   45
To what this ten yeares tribute will amount
That we have cast, but cannot compasse it
By reason of the warres, that robb'd our store;
And therefore are we to request your ayd.
BARABAS. Alas, my Lord, we are no souldiers: 50
And what's our aid against so great a Prince?
1 KNIGHT. Tut, Jew, we know thou art no souldier;
Thou art a Merchant, and a monied man,
And 'tis thy mony, *Barabas*, we seeke.
BARABAS. How, my Lord, my mony?
GOVERNOR.   Thine and the rest.   55
For to be short, amongst you 'tmust be had.
1 JEW. Alas, my Lord, the most of us are poore!
GOVERNOR. Then let the rich increase your portions:
BARABAS. Are strangers with your tribute to be tax'd?
2 KNIGHT. Have strangers leave with us to get their wealth?   60
Then let them with us contribute.
BARABAS. How, equally?
GOVERNOR.   No, Jew, like infidels.
For through our sufferance of your hatefull lives,
Who stand accursed in the sight of heaven,
These taxes and afflictions are befal'ne,   65
And therefore thus we are determined;
Reade there the Articles of our decrees.
READER. First, the tribute mony of the Turkes shall all be

    levyed amongst the Jewes, and each of them to pay one
    halfe of his estate.   70
BARABAS. How, halfe his estate? I hope you meane not mine.
GOVERNOR. Read on.
READER. Secondly, hee that denies to pay, shal straight
    become a Christian.
BARABAS. How a Christian? Hum, what's here to doe?   75
READER. Lastly, he that denies this, shall absolutely lose
    al he has.
ALL THREE JEWES. Oh my Lord we will give halfe.
BARABAS. Oh earth-mettall'd villaines, and no Hebrews born!
    And will you basely thus submit your selves   80
    To leave your goods to their arbitrament?
    GOVERNOR. Why *Barabas* wilt thou be christned?
BARABAS. No, Governour, I will be no convertite.
GOVERNOR. Then pay thy halfe.
BARABAS. Why know you what you doe by this device?   85
    Halfe of my substance is a Cities wealth.
    Governour, it was not got so easily;
    Nor will I part so slightly therewithall.
GOVERNOR. Sir, halfe is the penalty of our decree,
    Either pay that, or we will seize on all.   90
BARABAS. *Corpo di dio*; stay, you shall have halfe,
    Let me be us'd but as my brethren are.
GOVERNOR. No, Jew, thou hast denied the Articles,
    And now it cannot be recall'd.   [*Exeunt* Officers.]
BARABAS. Will you then steale my goods?   95
    Is theft the ground of your Religion?
GOVERNOR. No, Jew, we take particularly thine
    To save the ruine of a multitude:
    And better one want for a common good,
    Then many perish for a private man: 100
    Yet *Barrabas* we will not banish thee,
    But here in *Malta*, where thou gotst thy wealth,
    Live still; and if thou canst, get more.
BARABAS. Christians; what, or how can I multiply?
    Of nought is nothing made.   105
I KNIGHT. From nought at first thou camst to little welth,

84 doe] *Shone*; did *Q*

From little unto more, from more to most:
If your first curse fall heavy on thy head,
And make thee poore and scorn'd of all the world,
'Tis not our fault, but thy inherent sinne.   110
BARABAS. What, bring you Scripture to confirm your
    wrongs?
Preach me not out of my possessions.
Some Jewes are wicked, as all Christians are: [*Aside.*]
But say the Tribe that I descended of
Were all in generall cast away for sinne,   115
Shall I be tryed by their transgression?
The man that dealeth righteously shall live:
And which of you can charge me otherwise?
GOVERNOR. Out wretched *Barabas*, sham'st thou not thus
To justifie thy selfe, as if we knew not   120
Thy profession? If thou rely upon thy righteousnesse,
Be patient and thy riches will increase.
Excesse of wealth is cause of covetousnesse:
And covetousnesse, oh 'tis a monstrous sinne.
BARABAS. I, but theft is worse: tush, take not from me then, 125
For that is theft; and if you rob me thus,
I must be forc'd to steale and compasse more.
1 KNIGHT. Grave Governor, list not to his exclames:
Convert his mansion to a Nunnery,
His house will harbour many holy Nuns.   130

Enter OFFICERS.

GOVERNOR. It shall be so: now Officers have you done?
OFFICER. I, my Lord, we have seiz'd upon the goods
And wares of *Barabas*, which being valued
Amount to more then all the wealth in *Malta*.
And of the other we have seized halfe.   135
GOVERNOR. Then wee'll take order for the residue.
BARABAS. Well then my Lord, say, are you satisfied?
You have my goods, my mony, and my wealth,
My ships, my store, and all that I enjoy'd;
And having all, you can request no more;   140
Unlesse your unrelenting flinty hearts

135 GOVERNOR] *no speech-prefix* Q

Suppresse all pitty in your stony breasts,
And now shall move you to bereave my life.
GOVERNOR. No, *Barabas*, to staine our hands with blood
Is farre from us and our profession.   145
BARABAS. Why I esteeme the injury farre lesse,
To take the lives of miserable men,
Then be the causers of their misery.
You have my wealth the labour of my life,
The comfort of mine age, my childrens hope,   150
And therefore ne're distinguish of the wrong.
GOVERNOR. Content thee, *Barabas*, thou hast nought but right.
BARABAS. Your extreme right does me exceeding wrong:
But take it to you i'th'devils name.
GOVERNOR. Come, let us in, and gather of these goods   155
The mony for this tribute of the Turke.
I KNIGHT. 'Tis necessary that be look'd unto:
For if we breake our day, we breake the league,
And that will prove but simple policie.   *Exeunt.*

[*Manent* BARABAS *and the three* JEWES.]

BARABAS. I, policie? that's their profession,   160
And not simplicity, as they suggest.
The plagues of *Egypt*, and the curse of heaven,
Earths barrennesse, and all mens hatred
Inflict upon them, thou great *Primus Motor.*
And here upon my knees, striking the earth,   165
I banne their souls to everlasting paines
And extreme tortures of the fiery deepe,
That thus have dealt with me in my distresse:
I JEW. Oh yet be patient, gentle *Barabas.*
BARABAS. Oh silly brethren, borne to see this day!   170
Why stand you thus unmov'd with my laments?
Why weepe you not to thinke upon my wrongs?
Why pine not I, and dye in this distresse?
I JEW. Why, *Barabas*, as hardly can we brooke
The cruell handling of our selves in this: 175
Thou seest they have taken halfe our goods.
BARABAS. Why did you yeeld to their extortion?
You were a multitude, and I but one,
And of me onely have they taken all.

1 JEW. Yet brother *Barabas* remember *Job*.   180
BARABAS. What tell you me of *Job*? I wot his wealth
  Was written thus: he had seven thousand sheepe,
  Three thousand Camels, and five hundred yoake
  Of labouring Oxen, and five hundred
  Shee Asses: but for every one of those,   185
  Had they beene valued at indifferent rate,
  I had at home, and in mine Argosie
  And other ships that came from *Egypt* last,
  As much as would have bought his beasts and him,
  And yet have kept enough to live upon;   190
  So that not he, but I may curse the day,
  Thy fatall birth-day, forlorne *Barabas*;
  And henceforth wish for an eternall night,
  That clouds of darkenesse may inclose my flesh,
  And hide these extreme sorrowes from mine eyes: 195
  For onely I have toyl'd to inherit here
  The months of vanity and losse of time,
  And painefull nights have bin appointed me.
2 JEW. Good *Barabas* be patient.
BARABAS.   I, I,
  Pray leave me in my patience. You·that   200
  Were ne're possest of wealth, are pleas'd with want.
  But give him liberty at least to mourne,
  That in a field amidst his enemies,
  Doth see his souldiers slaine, himselfe disarm'd,
  And knowes no meanes of his recoverie: 205
  I, let me sorrow for this sudden chance,
  'Tis in the trouble of my spirit I speake;
  Great injuries are not so soone forgot.
1 JEW. Come, let us leave him in his irefull mood,
  Our words will but increase his extasie.   210
2 JEW. On then: but trust me 'tis a misery
  To see a man in such affliction:
  Farewell *Barabas*.   *Exeunt.*
BARABAS.   I, fare you well.
  See the simplicitie of these base slaves,
  Who for the villaines have no wit themselves,   215

182 five] *conj. Bawcutt;* two Q

Thinke me to be a senselesse lumpe of clay
That will with every water wash to dirt:
No, *Barabas* is borne to better chance,
And fram'd of finer mold then common men,
That measure nought but by the present time.   220
A reaching thought will search his deepest wits,
And cast with cunning for the time to come:
For evils are apt to happen every day.
But whither wends my beauteous *Abigall*?

      Enter ABIGALL *the Jewes daughter.*

Oh what has made my lovely daughter sad?   225
What? woman, moane not for a little losse:
Thy father has enough in store for thee.
ABIGALL. Not for my selfe, but aged *Barabas*:
Father, for thee lamenteth *Abigaile*:
But I will learne to leave these fruitlesse teares.   230
And urg'd thereto with my afflictions,
With fierce exclaimes run to the Senate-house,
And in the Senate reprehend them all,
And rent their hearts with tearing of my haire,
Till they reduce the wrongs done to my father.   235
BARABAS. No, *Abigail*, things past recovery
Are hardly cur'd with exclamations.
Be silent, Daughter, sufferance breeds ease,
And time may yeeld us an occasion
Which on the sudden cannot serve the turne.   240
Besides, my girle, thinke me not all so fond
As negligently to forgoe so much
Without provision for thy selfe and me.
Ten thousand Portagues, besides great Perles,
Rich costly Jewels, and Stones infinite,   245
Fearing the worst of this before it fell,
I closely hid.
ABIGALL.   Where father?
BARABAS.   In my house my girle.
ABIGALL. Then shall they ne're be seene of *Barrabas*:
For they have seiz'd upon thy house and wares.
BARABAS. But they will give me leave once more, I trow,   250
To goe into my house.

ABIGALL.   That may they not:
  For there I left the Governour placing Nunnes,
  Displacing me; and of thy house they meane
  To make a Nunnery, where none but their owne sect
  Must enter in; men generally barr'd.   255
BARABAS. My gold, my gold, and all my wealth is gone.
  You partiall heavens, have I deserv'd this plague?
  What will you thus oppose me, lucklesse Starres,
  To make me desperate in my poverty?
  And knowing me impatient in distresse   260
  Thinke me so mad as I will hang my selfe,
  That I may vanish ore the earth in ayre,
  And leave no memory that e're I was.
  No, I will live; nor loath I this life:
  And since you leave me in the Ocean thus   265
  To sinke or swim, and put me to my shifts,
  I'le rouse my senses, and awake my selfe.
  Daughter, I have it: thou perceiv'st the plight
  Wherein these Christians have oppressed me:
  Be rul'd by me, for in extremitie   270
  We ought to make barre of no policie.
ABIGALL. Father, what e're it be to injure them
  That have so manifestly wronged us,
  What will not *Abigall* attempt?
BARABAS.   Why so;
  Then thus, thou toldst me they have turn'd my house   275
  Into a Nunnery, and some Nuns are there.
ABIGALL. I did.
BARABAS.   Then *Abigall*, there must my girle
  Intreate the Abbasse to be entertain'd.
ABIGALL. How, as a Nunne?
BARABAS.   I, Daughter, for Religion
  Hides many mischiefes from suspition.   280
ABIGALL. I, but father they will suspect me there.
BARABAS. Let 'em suspect, but be thou so precise
  As they may thinke it done of Holinesse.
  Intreat 'em faire, and give them friendly speech,
  And seeme to them as if thy sinnes were great,   285
  Till thou hast gotten to be entertain'd.
ABIGALL. Thus father shall I much dissemble.

BARABAS. Tush, as good dissemble that thou never mean'st
  As first meane truth and then dissemble it,
  A counterfet profession is better   290
  Then unseene hypocrisie.
ABIGALL. Well father, say I be entertain'd,
  What then shall follow?
BARABAS.   This shall follow then;
  There have I hid close underneath the plancke
  That runs along the upper chamber floore,   295
  The gold and Jewels which I kept for thee.
  But here they come; be cunning *Abigall*.
ABIGALL. Then father goe with me.
BARABAS.   No, *Abigall*, in this
  It is not necessary I be seene,
  For I will seeme offended with thee for't.   300
  Be close, my girle, for this must fetch my gold.

      Enter two FRYARS *and two* NUNS.

1 FRYAR. Sisters, we now are almost at the new made Nunnery.
ABBASSE. The better; for we love not to be seene:
  'Tis thirtie winters long since some of us
  Did stray so farre amongst the multitude.   305
1 FRYAR. But, Madam, this house
  And waters of this new made Nunnery
  Will much delight you:
ABBASSE. It may be so: but who comes here?
ABIGALL. Grave Abbasse, and you happy Virgins guide,   310
  Pitty the state of a distressed Maid.
ABBASSE. What art thou, daughter?
ABIGALL. The hopelesse daughter of a haplesse *Jew*,
  The *Jew* of *Malta*, wretched *Barabas*;
  Sometimes the owner of a goodly house,   315
  Which they have now turn'd to a Nunnery.
ABBASSE. Well, daughter, say, what is thy suit with us?
ABIGALL. Fearing the afflictions which my father feeles,
  Proceed from sinne, or want of faith in us,
  I'de passe away my life in penitence,   320

And be a Novice in your Nunnery,
To make attonement for my labouring soule.

1 FRYAR. No doubt, brother, but this proceedeth of the spirit.

2 FRYAR. I, and of a moving spirit too, brother; but come,
Let us intreat she may be entertain'd. 325

ABBASSE. Well, daughter, we admit you for a Nun.

ABIGALL. First let me as a Novice learne to frame
My solitary life to your streight lawes,
And let me lodge where I was wont to lye.
I doe not doubt by your divine precepts 330
And mine owne industry, but to profit much.

BARABAS. As much I hope as all I hid is worth. *Aside.*

ABBASSE. Come daughter, follow us.

BARABAS. Why how now *Abigall*,
What mak'st thou amongst these hateful Christians?

1 FRYAR. Hinder her not, thou man of little faith, 335
For she has mortified her selfe.

BARABAS. How, mortified!

1 FRYAR. And is admitted to the Sister-hood.

BARABAS. Child of perdition, and thy fathers shame,
What wilt thou doe among these hatefull fiends?
I charge thee on my blessing that thou leave 340
These divels, and their damned heresie.

ABIGALL. Father give me—

BARABAS. Nay backe, *Abigall*,
And thinke upon the Jewels and the gold, *Whispers to her.*
The boord is marked thus † that covers it. [*Makes sign.*]
Away accursed from thy fathers sight. 345

1 FRYAR. *Barabas*, although thou art in mis-beleefe,
And wilt not see thine own afflictions,
Yet let thy daughter be no longer blinde.

BARABAS. Blind, Fryer, I wrecke not thy perswasions.
The boord is marked thus † that covers it, [*Aside, makes sign.*]
For I had rather dye, then see her thus. 351
Wilt thou forsake me too in my distresse,
Seduced Daughter, Goe forget not. *Aside to her.*
Becomes it Jewes to be so credulous,
To morrow early Il'e be at the doore. *Aside to her.*
No come not at me, if thou wilt be damn'd, 356
Forget me, see me not, and so be gone.

Farewell, Remember to morrow morning.   *Aside.*
Out, out thou wretch.

                            [*Exeunt, different ways.*]

[*Scaena* 3.]

MATHIAS. Whose this?
  Faire *Abigall* the rich Jewes daughter
  Become a Nun, her fathers sudden fall
  Has humbled her and brought her downe to this.
  Tut, she were fitter for a tale of love   5
  Then to be tired out with Orizons:
  And better would she farre become a bed
  Embraced in a friendly lovers armes,
  Then rise at midnight to a solemne masse.

Enter LODOWICKE.

LODOWICKE. Why how now Don *Mathias*, in a dump?   10
MATHIAS. Beleeve me, Noble *Lodowicke*, I have seene
  The strangest sight, in my opinion,
  That ever I beheld.
LODOWICKE.   What wast I prethe?
MATHIAS. A faire young maid scarce fourteene yeares of age,
  The sweetest flower in *Citherea's* field,   15
  Cropt from the pleasures of the fruitfull earth,
  And strangely metamorphis'd Nun.
LODOWICKE. But say, What was she?
MATHIAS.   Why the rich Jewes
  daughter.
LODOWICKE. What *Barabas*, whose goods were lately seiz'd?
  Is she so faire?
MATHIAS.   And matchlesse beautifull;   20
  As had you seene her 'twould have mov'd your heart,
  Tho countermur'd with walls of brasse, to love,
  Or at the least to pitty.
LODOWICKE. And if she be so faire as you report,
  'Twere time well spent to goe and visit her: 25
  How say you, shall we?
MATHIAS. I must and will, Sir, there's no remedy.

22 countermur'd] *conj. Collier*; countermin'd *Q*

LODOWICKE. And so will I too, or it shall goe hard.   [*Aside.*]
  Farewell *Mathias.*

MATHIAS.   Farewell *Lodowicke.*   *Exeunt.*

Actus Secundus [Scaena 1].

Enter BARABAS *with a light.*

BARABAS. Thus like the sad presaging Raven that tolls
    The sicke mans passeport in her hollow beake,
    And in the shadow of the silent night
    Doth shake contagion from her sable wings;
    Vex'd and tormented runnes poore *Barabas*   5
    With fatall curses towards these Christians.
    The incertaine pleasures of swift-footed time
    Have tane their flight, and left me in despaire;
    And of my former riches rests no more
    But bare remembrance; like a souldiers skarre,   10
    That has no further comfort for his maime.
    Oh thou that with a fiery piller led'st
    The sonnes of *Israel* through the dismall shades,
    Light *Abrahams* off-spring; and direct the hand
    Of *Abigall* this night; or let the day   15
    Turne to eternall darkenesse after this:
    No sleepe can fasten on my watchfull eyes,
    Nor quiet enter my distemper'd thoughts,
    Till I have answer of my *Abigall.*

Enter ABIGALL *above.*

ABIGALL. Now have I happily espy'd a time   20
    To search the plancke my father did appoint;
    And here behold (unseene) where I have found
    The gold, the perles, and Jewels which he hid.
BARABAS. Now I remember those old womens words,
    Who in my wealth wud tell me winters tales,   25
    And speake of spirits and ghosts that glide by night
    About the place where Treasure hath bin hid:
    And now me thinkes that I am one of those:
    For whilst I live, here lives my soules sole hope,
    And when I dye, here shall my spirit walke.   30
ABIGALL. Now that my fathers fortune were so good
    As but to be about this happy place;
    'Tis not so happy: yet when we parted last,

He said he wud attend me in the morne.
Then, gentle sleepe, where e're his bodie rests,   35
Give charge to *Morpheus* that he may dreame
A golden dreame, and of the sudden walke,
Come and receive the Treasure I have found.
BARABAS. *Bien para todos mi ganada no es*:
As good goe on, as sit so sadly thus.   40
But stay, what starre shines yonder in the East?
The Loadstarre of my life, if *Abigall*.
Who's there?
ABIGALL.   Who's that?
BARABAS.   Peace, *Abigal*, 'tis I.
ABIGALL. Then father here receive thy happinesse.
BARABAS. Hast thou't?
ABIGALL.   Here,   *Throwes downe bags.*
    Hast thou't? There's more,
   and more, and more.   45
BARABAS. Oh my girle,
My gold, my fortune, my felicity;
Strength to my soule, death to mine enemy;
Welcome the first beginner of my blisse:
Oh *Abigal*, *Abigal*, that I had thee here too,   50
Then my desires were fully satisfied,
But I will practise thy enlargement thence:
O girle, oh gold, oh beauty, oh my blisse!   *hugs his bags.*
ABIGALL. Father, it draweth towards midnight now,
And 'bout this time the Nuns begin to wake;
To shun suspition, therefore, let us part.   55
BARABAS. Farewell my joy, and by my fingers take
A kisse from him that sends it from his soule.
         [*Exit* ABIGALL.]
Now *Phoebus* ope the eye-lids of the day,
And for the Raven wake the morning Larke,   60
That I may hover with her in the Ayre;
Singing ore these, as she does ore her young.
Hermoso Placer, de los Dineros.   *Exit.*

[*Scaena* 2.]

Enter GOVERNOR, MARTIN DEL BOSCO,
the KNIGHTS [*and* OFFICERS].

GOVERNOR. Now Captaine tell us whither thou art bound?
  Whence is thy ship that anchors in our Rhoad?
  And why thou cam'st ashore without our leave?
BOSCO. Governor of *Malta*, hither am I bound;
  My Ship, *the flying Dragon*, is of *Spaine*,   5
  And so am I, *Delbosco* is my name;
  Vizadmirall unto the Catholike King.
1 KNIGHT. 'Tis true, my Lord, therefore intreat him well.
BOSCO. Our fraught is Grecians, Turks, and Africk Moores.
  For late upon the coast of *Corsica*,   10
  Because we vail'd not to the Turkish Fleet,
  Their creeping Gallyes had us in the chase:
  But suddenly the wind began to rise,
  And then we luft, and tackt, and fought at ease:
  Some have we fir'd, and many have we sunke;   15
  But one amongst the rest became our prize:
  The Captain's slaine, the rest remains our slaves,
  Of whom we would make sale in *Malta* here.
GOVERNOR. *Martin del Bosco*, I have heard of thee;
  Welcome to *Malta*, and to all of us;   20
  But to admit a sale of these thy Turkes
  We may not, nay we dare not give consent
  By reason of a Tributary league.
1 KNIGHT. *Delbosco*, as thou lovest and honour'st us,
  Perswade our Governor against the Turke;   25
  This truce we have is but in hope of gold,
  And with that summe he craves might we wage warre.
BOSCO. Will Knights of *Malta* be in league with Turkes,
  And buy it basely too for summes of gold?
  My Lord, Remember that to *Europ's* shame,   30
  The Christian Ile of *Rhodes*, from whence you came,
  Was lately lost, and you were stated here
  To be at deadly enmity with Turkes.

---

11 Turkish] *Scott*; *Spanish Q*   14 luft, and tackt] *Dyce*; left, and tooke *Q*

GOVERNOR. Captaine we know it, but our force is small.
BOSCO. What is the summe that *Calymath* requires?   35
GOVERNOR. A hundred thousand Crownes.
BOSCO. My Lord and King hath title to this Isle,
  And he meanes quickly to expell them hence;
  Therefore be rul'd by me, and keepe the gold:
  I'le write unto his Majesty for ayd,   40
  And not depart untill I see you free.
GOVERNOR. On this condition shall thy Turkes be sold.
  Goe Officers and set them straight in shew.

                        [*Exeunt* OFFICERS.]
  Bosco, thou shalt be *Malta's* Generall;
  We and our warlike Knights will follow thee   45
  Against these barbarous mis-beleeving Turkes.
BOSCO. So shall you imitate those you succeed:
  For when their hideous force inviron'd *Rhodes*,
  Small though the number was that kept the Towne,
  They fought it out, and not a man surviv'd   50
  To bring the haplesse newes to Christendome.
GOVERNOR. So will we fight it out; come let's away:
  Proud-daring *Calymath*, instead of gold,
  We'll send thee bullets wrapt in smoake and fire:
  Claime tribute where thou wilt, we are resolv'd,   55
  Honor is bought with bloud and not with gold.   *Exeunt.*

       38 them] *Scott*; you *Q*   54 thee] *Reed*; the *Q*

[*Scaena* 3.]

Enter OFFICERS *with* SLAVES.

1 OFFICER. This is the Market-place, here let 'em stand:
  Feare not their sale, for they'll be quickly bought.
2 OFFICER. Every ones price is written on his backe,
  And so much must they yeeld or not be sold.
1 OFFICER. Here comes the Jew, had not his goods bin seiz'd, 5
  He'de give us present mony for them all.

Enter BARABAS.

BARABAS. In spite of these swine-eating Christians,
  (Unchosen Nation, never circumciz'd;
  Such as poore villaines were ne're thought upon
  Till *Titus* and *Vespasian* conquer'd us.)   10
  Am I become as wealthy as I was:
  They hop'd my daughter would ha bin a Nun;
  But she's at home, and I have bought a house
  As great and faire as is the Governors;
  And there in spite of *Malta* will I dwell: 15
  Having *Fernezes* hand, whose heart I'le have;
  I, and his sonnes too, or it shall goe hard.
  I am not of the tribe of *Levy*, I,
  That can so soone forget an injury.
  We Jewes can fawne like Spaniels when we please;   20
  And when we grin we bite, yet are our lookes
  As innocent and harmelesse as a Lambes.
  I learn'd in *Florence* how to kisse my hand,
  Heave up my shoulders when they call me dogge,
  And ducke as low as any bare-foot Fryar,   25
  Hoping to see them starve upon a stall,
  Or else be gather'd for in our Synagogue;
  That when the offering-Bason comes to me,
  Even for charity I may spit intoo't.
  Here comes Don *Lodowicke* the Governor's sonne,   30
  One that I love for his good fathers sake.

Enter LODOWICKE.

LODOWICKE. I heare the wealthy Jew walked this way;
　　I'le seeke him out, and so insinuate,
　　That I may have a sight of *Abigall*;
　　For Don *Mathias* tels me she is faire.　　　　35
BARABAS. Now will I shew my selfe to have more of the
　　Serpent then the Dove; that is, more knave than foole.
　　　　　　　　　　　　　　　　　　　　　[*aside.*]
LODOWICKE. Yond walks the Jew, now for faire *Abigall*.
BARABAS. I, I, no doubt but shee's at your command.　[*aside.*]
LODOWICKE. *Barabas*, thou know'st I am the Governors
　　sonne.　　　　　　　　　　　　　　　　　　40
BARABAS. I wud you were his father too, Sir, thats al the
　　　　harm I wish you: the slave looks like a hogs cheek
　　　　new sindg'd.　　　　　　　　　　　　　[*aside.*]
LODOWICKE. Whither walk'st thou *Barabas*?
BARABAS. No further: 'tis a custome held with us,　　45
　　That when we speake with Gentiles like to you,
　　We turne into the Ayre to purge our selves:
　　For unto us the Promise doth belong.
LODOWICKE. Well, *Barabas*, canst helpe me to a Diamond?
BARABAS. Oh, Sir, your father had my Diamonds.　　50
　　Yet I have one left that will serve your turne:
　　I meane my daughter:—but e're he shall have her
　　I'le sacrifice her on a pile of wood.　　　　*aside.*
　　I ha the poyson of the City for him,
　　And the white leprosie.　　　　　　　　　55
LODOWICKE. What sparkle does it give without a foile?
BARABAS. The Diamond that I talke of, ne'r was foil'd:
　　But when he touches it, it will be foild:　　[*aside.*]
　　Lord *Lodowicke*, it sparkles bright and faire.
LODOWICKE. Is it square or pointed, pray let me know.　60
BARABAS. Pointed it is, good Sir,—but not for you.　*aside.*
LODOWICKE. I like it much the better.
BARABAS.　　　　　　　　　　So doe I too.
LODOWICKE. How showes it by night?
BARABAS.　　　　　　　　　　Outshines *Cinthia's* rayes:
　　You'le like it better farre a nights than dayes.　　*aside.*
LODOWICKE. And what's the price?　　　　　65
BARABAS. Your life and if you have it. [*aside.*]—Oh my Lord
　　We will not jarre about the price; come to my house

And I will giv't your honour—with a vengeance.   *aside.*
LODOWICKE. No, *Barabas*, I will deserve it first.
BARABAS. Good Sir, your father has deserv'd it at my hands,   70
Who of meere charity and Christian ruth,
To bring me to religious purity,
And as it were in Catechising sort,
To make me mindfull of my mortall sinnes,
Against my will, and whether I would or no,   75
Seiz'd all I had, and thrust me out a doores,
And made my house a place for Nuns most chast.
LODOWICKE. No doubt your soule shall reape the fruit of it.
BARABAS. I, but my Lord, the harvest is farre off:
And yet I know the prayers of those Nuns   80
And holy Fryers, having mony for their paines,
Are wondrous; and indeed doe no man good: *aside.*
And seeing they are not idle, but still doing,
'Tis likely they in time may reape some fruit,
I meane in fulnesse of perfection.   85
LODOWICKE. Good *Barabas* glance not at our holy Nuns.
BARABAS. No, but I doe it through a burning zeale,
Hoping ere long to set the house a fire;
For though they doe a while increase and multiply,   *aside.*
I'le have a saying to that Nunnery.   90
As for the Diamond, Sir, I told you of,
Come home and there's no price shall make us part,
Even for your Honourable fathers sake.
It shall goe hard but I will see your death,   *aside.*
But now I must be gone to buy a slave.   95
LODOWICKE. And, *Barabas*, I'le beare thee company.
BARABAS. Come then, here's the marketplace; whats the
price of this slave, two hundred Crowns? Do the
Turkes weigh so much?
1 OFFICER. Sir, that's his price.   100
BARABAS. What, can he steale that you demand so much?
Belike he has some new tricke for a purse;
And if he has, he is worth three hundred plats.
So that, being bought, the Towne-seale might be got
To keepe him for his life time from the gallowes.   105
The Sessions day is criticall to theeves,

And few or none scape but by being purg'd.

LODOWICKE. Ratest thou this Moore but at two hundred plats?

I OFFICER. No more, my Lord.

BARABAS. Why should this Turke be dearer then that Moore?

I OFFICER. Because he is young and has more qualities.   111

BARABAS. What, hast the Philosophers stone? and thou
    hast, breake my head with it, I'le forgive thee.

SLAVE. No Sir, I can cut and shave.

BARABAS. Let me see, sirra, are you not an old shaver?   115

SLAVE. Alas, Sir, I am a very youth.

BARABAS. A youth? I'le buy you, and marry you to Lady
    Vanity if you doe well.

SLAVE. I will serve you, Sir.

BARABAS. Some wicked trick or other. It may be under   120
    colour of shaving, thou'lt cut my throat for my
    goods. Tell me, hast thou thy health well?

SLAVE. I, passing well.

BARABAS. So much the worse; I must have one that's
    sickly, and be but for sparing vittles: 'tis not a stone   125
    of beef a day will maintaine you in these chops; let
    me see one that's somewhat leaner.

I OFFICER. Here's a leaner, how like you him?

BARABAS. Where was thou borne?

ITHIMORE. In *Trace*; brought up in *Arabia*.   130

BARABAS. So much the better, thou art for my turne,
    An hundred Crownes, I'le have him; there's the coyne.

I OFFICER. Then marke him, Sir, and take him hence.

BARABAS. I, marke him, you were best, for this is he
    That by my helpe shall doe much villanie.   [*aside.*]
    My Lord farewell: Come Sirra you are mine.   136
    As for the Diamond it shall be yours;
    I pray, Sir, be no stranger at my house,
    All that I have shall be at your command.

                                        [*Exit* LODOWICKE.]

                    Enter MATHIAS, MATER.

MATHIAS. What makes the Jew and *Lodowicke* so private?   140
    I feare me 'tis about faire *Abigall*.

BARABAS. Yonder comes Don *Mathias*, let us stay;

                    113, 115, 118, 122 SLAVE] *Ith.* Q

He loves my daughter, and she holds him deare:
But I have sworne to frustrate both their hopes,
And be reveng'd upon the—Governor.   [*aside.*]
MATER. This Moore is comeliest, is he not? speake son.   146
MATHIAS. No, this is the better, mother, view this well.
BARABAS. Seeme not to know me here before your mother
    Lest she mistrust the match that is in hand:
    When you have brought her home, come to my house;   150
    Thinke of me as thy father; Sonne farewell.
MATHIAS. But wherefore talk'd Don *Lodowick* with you?
BARABAS. Tush man, we talk'd of Diamonds, not of *Abigal.*
MATER. Tell me, *Mathias,* is not that the Jew?
BARABAS. As for the Comment on the *Machabees*   155
    I have it, Sir, and 'tis at your command.
MATHIAS. Yes, Madam, and my talke with him was but
    About the borrowing of a booke or two.
MATER. Converse not with him, he is cast off from heaven.
    Thou hast thy Crownes, fellow, come let's away.   160
MATHIAS. Sirra, Jew, remember the booke.   *exeunt.*
BARABAS.   Marry will I, Sir.
I OFFICER. Come, I have made a reasonable market,
    let's away.   [*Exeunt* Officers *and* Slaves.]
BARABAS. Now let me know thy name, and therewithall
    Thy birth, condition, and profession.   165
ITHIMORE. Faith, Sir, my birth is but meane, my name's
    Ithimer, my profession what you please.
BARABAS. Hast thou no Trade? then listen to my words,
    And I will teach thee that shall sticke by thee:
    First be thou voyd of these affections,   170
    Compassion, love, vaine hope, and hartlesse feare,
    Be mov'd at nothing, see thou pitty none,
    But to thy selfe smile when the Christians moane.
ITHIMORE. Oh brave, master, I worship your nose for this.
BARABAS. As for my selfe, I walke abroad a nights   175
    And kill sicke people groaning under walls:
    Sometimes I goe about and poyson wells;
    And now, and then, to Cherish Christian theeves,
    I am content to lose some of my Crownes;

156 but] *add. Dyce*   168 teach thee] *Reid*; teach *Q*

That I may, walking in my Gallery,   180
See 'em goe pinion'd along by my doore.
Being young I studied Physicke, and began
To practise first upon the Italian;
There I enrich'd the Priests with burials,
And always kept the Sexton's armes in ure   185
With digging graves and ringing dead mens knels:
And after that was I an Engineere,
And in the warres 'twixt *France* and *Germanie*,
Under pretence of helping *Charles* the fifth,
Slew friend and enemy with my strategems.   190
Then after that was I an Usurer,
And with extorting, cozening, forfeiting,
And tricks belonging unto Brokery,
I fill'd the Jailes with Bankrouts in a yeare,
And with young Orphans planted Hospitals,   195
And every Moone made some or other mad,
And now and then one hang himselfe for griefe,
Pinning upon his breast a long great Scrowle
How I with interest tormented him.
But marke how I am blest for plaguing them,   200
I have as much coyne as will buy the Towne.
But tell me now, How hast thou spent thy time?
ITHIMORE. Faith, Master,
In setting Christian villages on fire,
Chaining of Eunuches, binding gally-slaves.   205
One time I was an Hostler in an Inne,
And in the night time secretly would I steale
To travellers Chambers, and there cut their throats:
Once at *Jerusalem*, where the pilgrims kneel'd,
I strowed powder on the Marble stones   210
And therewithall their knees would ranckle, so
That I have laugh'd agood to see the cripples
Goe limping home to Christendome on stilts.
BARABAS. Why this is something: make account of me
As of thy fellow; we are villaines both: 215
Both circumcized, we hate Christians both:
Be true and secret, thou shalt want no gold.
But stand aside, here comes Don *Lodowicke*.

Enter LODOWICKE.

LODOWICKE. Oh *Barabas* well met; where is the Diamond
  You told me of?   220
BARABAS. I have it for you, Sir; please you walke in with
  me: What, ho, *Abigall*; open the doore I say.

Enter ABIGALL.

ABIGALL. In good time, father, here are letters come
  From *Ormus*, and the Post stayes here within.
BARABAS. Give me the letters, daughter, doe you heare?   225
  Entertaine *Lodowicke* the Governors sonne
  With all the curtesie you can affoord;
  Provided, that you keepe your Maiden-head.
  Use him as if he were a Philistine.   *aside.*
  Dissemble, sweare, protest, vow to love him,   230
  He is not of the seed of *Abraham*.
  I am a little busie, Sir, pray pardon me,
  Abigall, bid him welcome for my sake.
ABIGALL. For your sake and his own he's welcome hither.
BARABAS. Daughter, a word more; kisse him, speake him faire,
                                                  [*aside.*]
  And like a cunning Jew so cast about,   236
  That ye be both made sure e're you come out.
ABIGALL. Oh father, Don *Mathias* is my love.
BARABAS. I know it: yet I say make love to him;
  Doe, it is requisite it should be so.   240
  Nay on my life it is my Factors hand,
  But goe you in, I'le thinke upon the account:

[*Exeunt* LODOWICKE *and* ABIGALL.]

  The account is made, for *Lodowicke* dyes.
  My Factor sends me word a Merchant's fled
  That owes me for a hundred Tun of Wine: 245
  I weigh it thus much; I have wealth enough.
  For now by this has he kist *Abigall*;
  For she vowes love to him, and hee to her.
  As sure as heaven rain'd Manna for the Jewes,
  So sure shall he and Don *Mathias* dye: 250
  His father was my chiefest enemie.
  Whither goes Don *Mathias*? stay a while.

Enter MATHIAS.

MATHIAS. Whither but to my faire love *Abigall?*

BARABAS. Thou know'st, and heaven can witnesse it is true,
    That I intend my daughter shall be thine.   255

MATHIAS. I, *Barabas*, or else thou wrong'st me much.

BARABAS. Oh heaven forbid I should have such a thought.
    Pardon me though I weepe; the Governors sonne
    Will, whether I will or no, have *Abigall*:
    He sends her letters, bracelets, jewels, rings.   260

MATHIAS. Does she receive them?

BARABAS. Shee? No, *Mathias*, no, but sends them backe,
    And when he comes, she lockes her selfe up fast;
    Yet through the key-hole will he talke to her,
    While she runs to the window looking out   265
    When you should come and hale him from the doore.

MATHIAS. Oh treacherous *Lodowicke*!

BARABAS. Even now as I came home, he slipt me in,
    And I am sure he is with *Abigall*.

MATHIAS. I'le rouze him thence.   270

BARABAS. Not for all *Malta*, therefore sheath your sword;
    If you love me, no quarrels in my house;
    But steale you in, and seeme to see him not;
    I'le give him such a warning e're he goes
    As he shall have small hopes of *Abigall*.   275
    Away, for here they come.

Enter LODOWICKE, ABIGALL.

MATHIAS. What hand in hand, I cannot suffer this.

BARABAS. *Mathias*, as thou lov'st me, not a word.

MATHIAS. Well, let it passe, another time shall serve.   *Exit.*

LODOWICKE. *Barabas*, is not that the widowes sonne?   280

BARABAS. I, and take heed, for he hath sworne your death.

LODOWICKE. My death? what is the base borne peasant mad?

BARABAS. No, no, but happily he stands in feare
    Of that which you, I thinke, ne're dreame upon,
    My daughter here, a paltry silly girle.   285

LODOWICKE. Why loves she Don *Mathias*?

BARABAS. Doth she not with her smiling answer you?

ABIGALL. He has my heart, I smile against my will.   [*aside.*]

LODOWICKE. *Barabas*, thou know'st I have lov'd thy
　　daughter long.
BARABAS. And so has she done you, even from a child.　　　290
LODOWICKE. And now I can no longer hold my minde.
BARABAS. Nor I the affection that I beare to you.
LODOWICKE. This is thy Diamond, tell me, shall I have it?
BARABAS. Win it, and weare it, it is yet unsoyl'd.
　　Oh but I know your Lordship wud disdaine　　　　　295
　　To marry with the daughter of a Jew:
　　And yet I'le give her many a golden crosse
　　With Christian posies round about the ring.
LODOWICKE. 'Tis not thy wealth, but her that I esteeme,
　　Yet crave I thy consent.　　　　　　　　　　　300
BARABAS. And mine you have, yet let me talke to her;
　　This off-spring of *Cain*, this Jebusite
　　That never tasted of the Passeover,
　　Nor e're shall see the land of *Canaan*,
　　Nor our *Messias* that is yet to come,　　　　　　*aside*.
　　This gentle Magot *Lodowicke* I meane,　　　　　306
　　Must be deluded: let him have thy hand,
　　But keep thy heart till Don *Mathias* comes.
ABIGALL. What shall I be betroth'd to *Lodowicke*?
BARABAS. It's no sinne to deceive a Christian;　　　　310
　　For they themselves hold it a principle,
　　Faith is not to be held with Heretickes;
　　But all are Hereticks that are not Jewes;
　　This followes well, and therefore daughter feare not.
　　I have intreated her, and she will grant.　　　　　315
LODOWICKE. Then gentle *Abigal* plight thy faith to me.
ABIGALL. I cannot chuse, ṣeeing my father bids:　　[*aside*.]
　　Nothing but death shall part my love and me.
LODOWICKE. Now have I that for which my soule hath long'd.
BARABAS. So have not I, but yet I hope I shall.　　*aside*.
ABIGALL. Oh wretched *Abigal*, what hast thou done?　　321
LODOWICKE. Why on the sudden is your colour chang'd?
ABIGALL. I know not, but farewell, I must be gone.
BARABAS. Stay her, but let her not speake one word more.
LODOWICKE. Mute a the sudden; here's a sudden change.　　325

319 thou] *Scott*; thee *Q*

BARABAS. Oh muse not at it, 'tis the Hebrewes guize,
　　That maidens new betroth'd should weepe a while:
　　Trouble her not, sweet *Lodowicke* depart:
　　Shee is thy wife, and thou shalt be mine heire.
LODOWICKE. Oh, is't the custome, then I am resolv'd:　　330
　　But rather let the brightsome heavens be dim,
　　And Natures beauty choake with stifeling clouds,
　　Then my faire *Abigal* should frowne on me.
　　There comes the villaine, now I'le be reveng'd.

　　　　　　　Enter MATHIAS.

BARABAS. Be quiet *Lodowicke*, it is enough　　335
　　That I have made thee sure to *Abigal*.
LODOWICKE. Well, let him goe.　　　　　　　*Exit*.
BARABAS. Well, but for me, as you went in at dores
　　You had bin stab'd, but not a word on't now;
　　Here must no speeches passe, nor swords be drawne.　　340
MATHIAS. Suffer me, *Barabas*, but to follow him.
BARABAS. No; so shall I, if any hurt be done,
　　Be made an accessary of your deeds;
　　Revenge it on him when you meet him next.
MATHIAS. For this I'le have his heart.　　　　　345
BARABAS. Doe so; loe here I give thee *Abigall*.
MATHIAS. What greater gift can poore *Mathias* have?
　　Shall *Lodowicke* rob me of so faire a love?
　　My life is not so deare as *Abigall*.
BARABAS. My heart misgives me, that to crosse your love,　　350
　　Hee's with your mother, therefore after him.
MATHIAS. What, is he gone unto my mother?
BARABAS. Nay, if you will, stay till she comes her selfe.
MATHIAS. I cannot stay; for if my mother come,
　　Shee'll dye with griefe.　　　　　　　　*Exit*.
ABIGALL. I cannot take my leave of him for teares:　　356
　　Father, why have you thus incenst them both?
BARABAS. What's that to thee?
ABIGALL.　　　　　　　　I'le make 'em friends againe.
BARABAS. You'll make 'em friends?
　　Are there not Jewes enow in *Malta*.　　　　360
　　But thou must dote upon a Christian?
ABIGALL. I will have Don *Mathias*, he is my love.

BARABAS. Yes, you shall have him: Goe put her in.

ITHIMORE. I, I'le put her in. [*Exit* ABIGALL.]

BARABAS. Now tell me, *Ithimore*, how lik'st thou this? 365

ITHIMORE. Faith Master, I thinke by this
You purchase both their lives; is it not so?

BARABAS. True; and it shall be cunningly perform'd.

ITHIMORE. Oh, master, that I might have a hand in this.

BARABAS. I, so thou shalt, 'tis thou must doe the deed: 370
Take this and beare it to *Mathias* streight,
And tell him that it comes from *Lodowicke*.

ITHIMORE. 'Tis poyson'd, is it not?

BARABAS. No, no, and yet it might be done that way:
It is a challenge feign'd from *Lodowicke*. 375

ITHIMORE. Feare not, I'le so set his heart a fire,
That he shall verily thinke it comes from him.

BARABAS. I cannot choose but like thy readinesse:
Yet be not rash, but doe it cunningly. 379

ITHIMORE. As I behave my selfe in this, imploy me hereafter.

BARABAS. Away then. *Exit.*
So, now will I goe in to *Lodowicke*,
And like a cunning spirit feigne some lye,
Till I have set 'em both at enmitie. *Exit.*

Actus Tertius [Scaena 1].

Enter a CURTEZANE.

CURTEZANE. Since this Towne was besieg'd, my gaine
    growes cold:
    The time has bin, that but for one bare night
    A hundred Duckets have bin freely given:
    But now against my will I must be chast.
    And yet I know my beauty doth not faile.   5
    From *Venice* Merchants, and from *Padua*
    Were wont to come rare witted Gentlemen,
    Schollers I meane, learned and liberall;
    And now, save *Pilia-borza*, comes there none,
    And he is very seldome from my house;   10
    And here he comes.

Enter PILIA-BORZA.

PILIA-BORZA. Hold thee, wench, there's something for
    thee to spend.
CURTEZANE. 'Tis silver, I disdaine it.
PILIA-BORZA. I, but the Jew has gold,
    And I will have it or it shall goe hard.   15
CURTEZANE. Tell me, how cam'st thou by this?
PILIA-BORZA. Faith, walking the backe lanes through the
    Gardens I chanc'd to cast mine eye up to the Jewes
    counting-house where I saw some bags of mony, and
    in the night I clamber'd up with my hooks, and as I   20
    was taking my choyce, I heard a rumbling in the
    house; so I tooke onely this, and runne my way: but
    here's the Jews man.

Enter ITHIMORE.

CURTEZANE. Hide the bagge.
PILIA-BORZA. Looke not towards him, let's away: Zoons   25
    what a looking thou keep'st, thou'lt betraye's anon.
                                    [Exeunt.]
ITHAMORE. O the sweetest face that ever I beheld! I
    know she is a Curtezane by her attire: now would I

give a hundred of the Jewes Crownes that I had such
a Concubine.   30

Well, I have deliver'd the challenge in such sort,
As meet they will, and fighting dye; brave sport.

Exit.

[*Scaena* 2.]

Enter MATHIAS.

MATHIAS. This is the place, now *Abigall* shall see
Whether *Mathias* holds her deare or no.

Enter LODOWICKE *reading.*

LODOWICKE. What, dares the villain write in such base terms?
MATHIAS. I did it, and revenge it if thou dar'st.

Fight: Enter BARABAS *above.*

BARABAS. Oh bravely fought, and yet they thrust not home.   5
Now *Lodowicke*, now *Mathias*, so;   [*Both fall.*]
So now they have shew'd themselves to be tall fellowes.
[VOICES] *within*, Part'em, part 'em.
BARABAS. I, part 'em now they are dead: Farewell, farewell.

Exit.

Enter GOVERNOR, MATER [*and* Attendants].

GOVERNOR. What sight is this? my *Lodowicke* slaine!   10
These armes of mine shall be thy Sepulchre.
MATER. Who is this? my sonne *Mathias* slaine!
GOVERNOR. Oh *Lodowicke*! hadst thou perish'd by the Turke,
Wretched *Ferneze* might have veng'd thy death.
MATER. Thy sonne slew mine, and I'le revenge his death.   15
GOVERNOR. Looke, *Katherin*, looke, thy sonne gave mine
these wounds.
MATER. O leave to grieve me, I am griev'd enough.
GOVERNOR. Oh that my sighs could turne to lively breath;
And these my teares to blood, that he might live.
MATER. Who made them enemies?   20
GOVERNOR. I know not, and that grieves me most of all.
MATER. My sonne lov'd thine.
GOVERNOR.   And so did *Lodowicke* him.
MATER. Lend me that weapon that did kill my sonne,
And it shall murder me.

GOVERNOR. Nay Madam stay, that weapon was my son's,   25
   And on that rather should *Ferneze* dye.
MATER. Hold, let's inquire the causers of their deaths,
   That we may venge their blood upon their heads.
GOVERNOR. Then take them up, and let them be interr'd
   Within one sacred monument of stone;   30
   Upon which Altar I will offer up
   My daily sacrifice of sighes and teares,
   And with my prayers pierce impartiall heavens,
   Till they reveal the causers of our smarts,
   Which forc'd their hands divide united hearts: 35
   Come, *Katherina*, our losses equall are,
   Then of true griefe let us take equall share.   *Exeunt.*

34 reveal] *add. Dyce*

[*Scaena* 3.]

Enter ITHIMORE.

ITHIMORE. Why was there ever seene such villany,
So neatly plotted, and so well perform'd?
Both held in hand, and flatly both beguil'd.

Enter ABIGALL.

ABIGALL. Why how now *Ithimore*, why laugh'st thou so?
ITHIMORE. Oh, Mistresse, ha ha ha.   5
ABIGALL. Why what ayl'st thou?
ITHIMORE. Oh my master.
ABIGALL. Ha.
ITHIMORE. Oh Mistris! I have the bravest, gravest,
    secret, subtil bottle-nos'd knave to my Master, that   10
    ever Gentleman had.
ABIGALL. Say, knave, why rail'st upon my father thus?
ITHIMORE. Oh, my master has the bravest policy.
ABIGALL. Wherein?
ITHIMORE. Why, know you not?   15
ABIGALL. Why no.
ITHIMORE. Know you not of *Mathias* and Don
    Lodowickes disaster?
ABIGALL. No, what was it?
ITHIMORE. Why the devil invented a challenge, my   20
    Master writ it, and I carried it, first to *Lodowicke*,
    and *imprimis* to *Mathias*.
And then they met, and as the story sayes,
In dolefull wise they ended both their dayes.
ABIGALL. And was my father furtherer of their deaths?   25
ITHIMORE. Am I *Ithimore*?
ABIGALL. Yes.
ITHIMORE. So sure did your father write, and I cary the
    chalenge.
ABIGALL. Well, *Ithimore*, let me request thee this,   30
Goe to the new made Nunnery, and inquire
For any of the Fryars of St *Jaques*,

23 and] *add. Chappell*

And say, I pray them come and speake with me.

ITHIMORE. I pray, mistris, wil you answer me to one question?

ABIGALL. Well, sirra, what is't?   35

ITHIMORE. A very feeling one; have not the Nuns fine
  sport with the Fryars now and then?

ABIGALL. Go to, sirra sauce, is this your question? get ye gon.

ITHIMORE. I will forsooth, Mistris.   *Exit.*

ABIGALL. Hard-hearted Father, unkind *Barabas*,   40
  Was this the pursuit of thy policie?
  To make me shew them favour severally,
  That by my favour they should both be slaine?
  Admit thou lov'dst not *Lodowicke* for his sire,
  Yet Don *Mathias* ne're offended thee: 45
  But thou wert set upon extreme revenge,
  Because the Pryor dispossest thee once,
  And couldst not venge it, but upon his sonne,
  Nor on his sonne, but by *Mathias* meanes;
  Nor on *Mathias*, but by murdering me.   50
  But I perceive there is no love on earth,
  Pitty in Jewes, nor piety in Turkes.
  But here comes cursed *Ithimore* with the Fryar.

Enter ITHIMORE, I FRYAR.

I FRYAR. *Virgo, salve.*

ITHIMORE. When ducke you?   55

ABIGALL. Welcome grave Fryar: *Ithamore* begon,
                                    Exit [ITHIMORE].
  Know, holy Sir, I am bold to sollicite thee.

I FRYAR. Wherein?

ABIGALL. To get me be admitted for a Nun.

I FRYAR. Why *Abigal* it is not yet long since   60
  That I did labour thy admition,
  And then thou didst not like that holy life.

ABIGALL. Then were my thoughts so fraile and unconfirm'd,
  And I was chain'd to follies of the world:
  But now experience, purchased with griefe,   65
  Has made me see the difference of things.
  My sinfull soule, alas, hath pac'd too long

39 sire] *Dyce*; sinne *Q*

The fatall Labyrinth of misbeleefe,
Farre from the Sonne that gives eternall life.
I FRYAR. Who taught thee this?
ABIGALL.   The Abbasse of the house,   70
Whose zealous admonition I embrace:
Oh therefore, *Jacomo*, let me be one,
Although unworthy of that Sister-hood.
I FRYAR. *Abigal* I will, but see thou change no more,
For that will be most heavy to thy soule.   75
ABIGALL. That was my father's fault.
I FRYAR.   Thy father's, how?
ABIGALL. Nay, you shall pardon me: oh Barabas,   [*aside.*]
Though thou deservest hardly at my hands,
Yet never shall these lips bewray thy life.   79
I FRYAR. Come, shall we goe?
ABIGALL.   My duty waits on you. *Exeunt.*

[*Scaena* 4.]

Enter BARABAS *reading a letter.*

BARABAS. What, *Abigall* become a Nunne again?
　False, and unkinde; what hast thou lost thy father?
　And all unknowne, and unconstrain'd of me,
　Art thou againe got to the Nunnery?
　Now here she writes, and wils me to repent.　　　　　　　5
　Repentance? *Spurca*: what pretendeth this?
　I feare she knowes ('tis so) of my device
　In Don *Mathias* and *Lodovicoes* deaths:
　If so, 'tis time that it be seene into:
　For she that varies from me in beleefe　　　　　　　　10
　Gives great presumption that she loves me not;
　Or loving, doth dislike of something done:
　But who comes here?

[*Enter* ITHIMORE.]

　　　　　　Oh *Ithimore* come neere;
　Come neere my love, come neere thy masters life,
　My trusty servant, nay, my second selfe;　　　　　　　15
　For I have now no hope but even in thee;
　And on that hope my happinesse is built:
　When saw'st thou *Abigall*?
ITHIMORE. To day.
BARABAS. With whom?　　　　　　　　　　　　　　　20
ITHIMORE. A Fryar.
BARABAS. A Fryar? false villaine, he hath done the deed.
ITHIMORE. How, Sir?
BARABAS. Why made mine *Abigall* a Nunne.
ITHIMORE. That's no lye, for she sent me for him.　　　25
BARABAS. Oh unhappy day,
　False, credulous, inconstant *Abigall*!
　But let 'em goe: And *Ithimore*, from hence
　Ne're shall she grieve me more with her disgrace;
　Ne're shall she live to inherit ought of mine,　　　　30
　Be blest of me, nor come within my gates,

15 selfe] *Penley*; life *Q*

But perish underneath my bitter curse
Like *Cain* by *Adam*, for his brother's death.
ITHIMORE. Oh master.
BARABAS. *Ithimore*, intreat not for her, I am mov'd,   35
    And she is hatefull to my soule and me:
    And least thou yeeld to this that I intreat,
    I cannot thinke but that thou hat'st my life.
ITHIMORE. Who I, master? Why I'le run to some rocke
    and throw my selfe headlong into the sea; why I'le   40
    doe any thing for your sweet sake.
BARABAS. Oh trusty *Ithimore*; no servant, but my friend;
    I here adopt thee for mine onely heire,
    All that I have is thine when I am dead,
    And whilst I live use halfe; spend as my selfe;   45
    Here take my keyes, I'le give 'em thee anon:
    Goe buy thee garments: but thou shalt not want:
    Onely know this, that thus thou art to doe:
    But first goe fetch me in the pot of Rice
    That for our supper stands upon the fire.   50
ITHIMORE. I hold my head my master's hungry: I goe Sir.

                                              Exit.

BARABAS. Thus every villaine ambles after wealth
    Although he ne're be richer then in hope:
    But hush't.

                Enter ITHIMORE *with the pot.*

ITHIMORE. Here 'tis, Master.   55
BARABAS. Well said, *Ithimore*; what hast thou brought
    the Ladle with thee too?
ITHIMORE. Yes, Sir, the proverb saies, he that eats with
    the devil had need of a long spoone, I have brought
    you a Ladle.   60
BARABAS. Very well, *Ithimore*, then now be secret;
    And for thy sake, whom I so dearely love,
    Now shalt thou see the death of *Abigall*,
    That thou mayst freely live to be my heire.
ITHIMORE. Why, master, wil you poison her with a   65
    messe of rice porredge that wil preserve life, make
    her round and plump, and batten more then you are
    aware.

BARABAS. I but *Ithimore* seest thou this?
 It is a precious powder that I bought   70
 Of an Italian in *Ancona* once,
 Whose operation is to binde, infect,
 And poyson deeply: yet not appeare
 In forty houres after it is tane.
ITHIMORE. How master?   75
BARABAS. Thus *Ithimore*:
 This Even they use in *Malta* here ('tis call'd
 Saint *Jaques* Even) and then I say they use
 To send their Almes unto the Nunneries:
 Among the rest beare this, and set it there;   80
 There's a darke entry where they take it in,
 Where they must neither see the messenger,
 Nor make enquiry who hath sent it them.
ITHIMORE. How so?
BARABAS. Belike there is some Ceremony in't.   85
 There *Ithimore* must thou goe place this pot:
 Stay, let me spice it first.
ITHIMORE. Pray doe, and let me help you Master. Pray
 let me taste first.
BARABAS. Prethe doe: what saist thou now?   90
ITHIMORE. Troth Master I'm loth such a pot of pottage
 should be spoyld.
BARABAS. Peace, *Ithimore*, 'tis better so then spar'd.
 Assure they selfe thou shalt have broth by the eye.
 My purse, my Coffer, and my selfe is thine.   95
ITHIMORE. Well, Master, I goe.
BARABAS. Stay, first let me stirre it *Ithimore*.
 As fatall be it to her as the draught
 Of which great *Alexander* drunke, and dyed:
 And with her let it worke like *Borgias* wine,   100
 Whereof his sire, the Pope, was poyson'd.
 In few, the blood of *Hydra*, *Lerna's* bane;
 The jouyce of Hebon, and *Cocitus* breath,
 And all the poysons of the Stygian poole
 Breake from the fiery kingdome; and in this   105
 Vomit your venome, and invenome her

85 pot] *Reed*; plot *Q*

That like a fiend hath left her father thus.

ITHIMORE. What a blessing has he given't? was ever pot
of rice porredge so sauc't? what shall I doe with it?

BARABAS. Oh my sweet *Ithimore* goe set it downe   110
And come againe so soone as thou hast done,
For I have other businesse for thee.

ITHIMORE. Heres a drench to poyson a whole stable of
Flanders mares: I'le carry't to the Nuns with a powder.   115

BARABAS. And the horse pestilence to boot; away.

ITHIMORE. I am gone.
Pay me my wages for my worke is done.   *Exit.*

BARABAS. Ile pay thee with a vengeance *Ithamore*.   *Exit.*

[*Scaena* 5.]

Enter GOVERNOR, BOSCO, Knights, BASSO.

GOVERNOR. Welcome great Bashaw, how fares *Callymath*,
   What wind drives you thus into *Malta* rhode?
BASSO. The wind that bloweth all the world besides,
   Desire of gold.
GOVERNOR.   Desire of gold, great Sir?
   That's to be gotten in the Westerne *Inde*:   5
   In *Malta* are no golden Minerals.
BASSO. To you of *Malta* thus saith *Calymath*:
   The time you tooke for respite, is at hand,
   For the performance of your promise past;
   And for the Tribute-mony I am sent.   10
GOVERNOR. Bashaw, in briefe, shalt have no tribute here,
   Nor shall the Heathens live upon our spoyle:
   First will we race the City wals our selves,
   Lay waste the Iland, hew the Temples downe,
   And shipping off our goods to *Sicily*,   15
   Open an entrance for the wastfull sea,
   Whose billowes beating the resistlesse bankes,
   Shall overflow it with their refluence.
BASSO. Well, Governor, since thou hast broke the league
   By flat denyall of the promis'd Tribute,   20
   Talke not of racing downe your City wals,
   You shall not need trouble your selves so farre,
   For *Selim-Calymath* shall come himselfe,
   And with brasse-bullets batter downe your Towers,
   And turne proud *Malta* to a wildernesse   25
   For these intolerable wrongs of yours;
   And so farewell.   [*Exit.*]
GOVERNOR.   Farewell:
   And now you men of *Malta* looke about,
   And let's provide to welcome *Calymath*;
   Close your Port-cullise, charge your Basiliskes,   30
   And as you profitably take up Armes,
   So now couragiously encounter them;

For by this Answer, broken is the league,
And nought is to be look'd for now but warres,
And nought to us more welcome is then warres.   35

Exeunt.

[*Scaena* 6.]

Enter two FRYARS.

1 FRYAR. Oh brother, brother, all the Nuns are sicke,
And Physicke will not helpe them; they must dye.

2 FRYAR. The Abbasse sent for me to be confest:
Oh what a sad confession will there be?

1 FRYAR. And so did faire *Maria* send for me: 5
I'le to her lodging; hereabouts she lyes.   *Exit.*

Enter ABIGALL.

2 FRYAR. What, all dead save onely *Abigall?*

ABIGALL. And I shall dye too, for I feele death comming.
Where is the Fryar that converst with me?

2 FRYAR. Oh he is gone to see the other Nuns.   10

ABIGALL. I sent for him, but seeing you are come
Be you my ghostly father; and first know,
That in this house I liv'd religiously,
Chast, and devout, much sorrowing for my sinnes,
But e're I came—   15

2 FRYAR. What then?

ABIGALL. I did offend high heaven so grievously,
As I am almost desperate for my sinnes:
And one offence torments me more then all.
You knew *Mathias* and Don *Lodowicke?*   20

2 FRYAR. Yes, what of them?

ABIGALL. My father did contract me to 'em both:
First to Don *Lodowicke,* him I never lov'd;
Mathias was the man that I held deare,
And for his sake did I become a Nunne.   25

2 FRYAR. So, say how was their end?

ABIGALL. Both jealous of my love, envied each other:
And by my father's practice, which is there   [*Gives paper.*]
Set downe at large, the Gallants were both slaine.

2 FRYAR. Oh monstrous villany: 30

ABIGALL. To worke my peace, this I confesse to thee;
Reveale it not, for then my father dyes.

2 FRYAR. Know that Confession must not be reveal'd,

The Canon Law forbids it, and the Priest
That makes it knowne, being degraded first,   35
Shall be condemn'd, and then sent to the fire.
ABIGALL. So I have heard; pray therefore keepe it close.
Death seizeth on my heart, ah gentle Fryar
Convert my father that he may be sav'd,
And witnesse that I dye a Christian.   [*Dies.*]
2 FRYAR. I, and a Virgin too, that grieves me most: 41
But I must to the Jew and exclaime on him,
And make him stand in feare of me.

Enter 1 FRYAR.

1 FRYAR. Oh brother, all the Nuns are dead, let's bury them.
2 FRYAR. First helpe to bury this, then goe with me   45
And helpe me to exclaime against the Jew.
1 FRYAR. Why? what has he done?
2 FRYAR. A thing that makes me tremble to unfold.
1 FRYAR. What has he crucified a child?
2 FRYAR. No, but a worse thing: 'twas told me in shrift,   50
Thou know'st 'tis death and if it be reveal'd.
Come let's away.   *Exeunt.*

Actus Quartus [*Scaena 1*].

Enter BARABAS, ITHIMORE.   *Bells within.*

BARABAS. There is no musicke to a Christians knell:
How sweet the Bels ring now the Nuns are dead
That sound at other times like Tinkers pans?
I was afraid the poyson had not wrought;
Or though it wrought, it would have done no good,   5
For every yeare they swell, and yet they live;
Now all are dead, not one remaines alive.
ITHIMORE. That's brave, Master, but think you it wil
    not be known?
BARABAS. How can it if we two be secret.   10
ITHIMORE. For my part feare you not.
BARABAS. I'de cut thy throat if I did.
ITHIMORE. And reason too;
    But here's a royall Monastry hard by,
Good master let me poyson all the Monks.   15
BARABAS. Thou shalt not need, for now the Nuns are dead,
    They'll dye with griefe.
ITHIMORE. Doe you not sorrow for your daughters death?
BARABAS. No, but I grieve because she liv'd so long
An Hebrew borne, and would become a Christian.   20
Cazzo diabolo.

Enter the two FRYARS.

ITHIMORE. Look, look, Master, here come two religious
    Caterpillers.
BARABAS. I smelt 'em e're they came.
ITHIMORE. God-a-mercy nose; come let's begone.   25
2 FRYAR. Stay wicked Jew, repent, I say, and stay:
1 FRYAR. Thou hast offended, therefore must be damn'd.
BARABAS. I feare they know we sent the poyson'd broth.
ITHIMORE. And so doe I, master, therefore speake 'em faire.
2 FRYAR. *Barabas,* thou hast—   30
1 FRYAR. I, that thou hast—
BARABAS. True, I have mony, what though I have?
2 FRYAR. Thou art a—

1 FRYAR. I, that thou art a—
BARABAS. What needs all this? I know I am a Jew.   35
2 FRYAR. Thy daughter—
1 FRYAR. I, thy daughter,—
BARABAS. Oh speake not of her, then I dye with griefe.
2 FRYAR. Remember that—
1 FRYAR. I, remember that—   40
BARABAS. I must needs say that I have beene a great usurer.
2 FRYAR. Thou hast committed—
BARABAS. Fornication? but that was in another Country:
    And besides, the Wench is dead.
2 FRYAR. I, but *Barabas* remember *Mathias* and Don   45
    Lodowick.
BARABAS. Why, what of them?
2 FRYAR. I will not say that by a forged challenge they met.
BARABAS. She has confest, and we are both undone;   [*Aside.*]
    My bosome inmates, but I must dissemble.   *aside.*
    Oh holy Fryars, the burthen of my sinnes   51
    Lye heavy on my soule; then pray you tell me,
    Is't not too late now to turne Christian?
    I have beene zealous in the Jewish faith,
    Hart harted to the poore, a covetous wretch,   55
    That would for Lucars sake have sold my soule.
    A hundred for a hundred I have tane;
    And now for store of wealth may I compare
    With all the Jewes in *Malta*; but what is wealth?
    I am a Jew, and therefore am I lost.   60
    Would pennance serve for this my sinne,
    I could afford to whip my selfe to death.
ITHIMORE. And so could I; but pennance will not serve.
BARABAS. To fast, to pray, and weare a shirt of haire,
    And on my knees creepe to *Jerusalem.*   65
    Cellers of Wine, and Sollers full of Wheat,
    Ware-houses stuft with spices and with drugs,
    Whole Chests of Gold, in Bullione, and in Coyne,
    Besides I know not how much weight in Pearle
    Orient and round, have I within my house;   70
    At *Alexandria*, Merchandize unsold:
    But yesterday two ships went from this Towne,
    Their voyage will be worth ten thousand Crownes.

In *Florence, Venice, Antwerpe, London, Civill,*
Frankeford, Lubecke, Mosco, and where not,   75
Have I debts owing; and in most of these,
Great summes of mony lying in the bancho;
All this I'le give to some religious house
So I may be baptiz'd and live therein.

1 FRYAR. Oh good *Barabas* come to our house.   80
2 FRYAR. Oh no, good *Barabas* come to our house.
And *Barabas,* you know—
BARABAS. I know that I have highly sinn'd,
 You shall convert me, you shall have all my wealth.
1 FRYAR. Oh *Barabas,* their Lawes are strict.   85
BARABAS. I know they are, and I will be with you.
2 FRYAR. They weare no shirts, and they goe bare-foot too.
BARABAS. Then 'tis not for me; and I am resolv'd
 You shall confesse me, and have all my goods.
1 FRYAR. Good *Barabas* come to me.   90
BARABAS. You see I answer him, and yet he stayes;
 Rid him away, and goe you home with me.
2 FRYAR. I'le be with you to night.
BARABAS. Come to my house at one a clocke this night.
1 FRYAR. You heare your answer, and you may be gone.   95
2 FRYAR. Why goe get you away.
1 FRYAR. I will not goe for thee.
2 FRYAR. No, then I'le make thee rogue.
1 FRYAR. How, dost call me rogue?   *Fight.*
ITHIMORE. Part 'em, master, part 'em.   100
BARABAS. This is meere frailty, brethren, be content.
 Fryar *Barnardine* goe you with *Ithimore.*
 You know my mind, let alone with him.   [*aside.*]

Exeunt [ITHIMORE *and* 2 FRYAR].

1 FRYAR. Why does he goe to thy house, let him begone.
BARABAS. I'le give him something and so stop his mouth.   105
I never heard of any man but he
Malign'd the order of the Jacobines:
But doe you thinke that I beleeve his words?
Why Brother you converted *Abigall*;

And I am bound in charitie to requite it,   110
And so I will, oh *Jacomo*, faile not but come.
1 FRYAR. But *Barabas* who shall be your godfathers,
  For presently you shall be shriv'd.
BARABAS. Marry the Turke shall be one of my godfa-
  thers,
But not a word to any of your Covent.   115
1 FRYAR. I warrant thee, *Barabas*.   *Exit.*
BARABAS. So now the feare is past, and I am safe:
  For he that shriv'd her is within my house,
  What if I murder'd him e're *Jacomo* comes?
  Now I have such a plot for both their lives,   120
  As never Jew nor Christian knew the like:
  One turn'd my daughter, therefore he shall dye;
  The other knowes enough to have my life,
  Therefore 'tis requisite he should not live.
  But are not both these wise men to suppose   125
  That I will leave my house, my goods, and all,
  To fast and be well whipt; I'le none of that.
  Now Fryar *Bernardine* I come to you,
  I'le feast you, lodge you, give you faire words,
  And after that, I and my trusty Turke—   130
  No more but so: it must and shall be done.
  Ithimore, tell me, is the Fryar asleepe?

Enter ITHIMORE.

ITHIMORE. Yes; and I know not what the reason is,
  Doe what I can he will not strip himselfe,
  Nor goe to bed, but sleepes in his owne clothes;   135
  I feare me he mistrusts what we intend.
BARABAS. No, 'tis an order which the Fryars use:
  Yet if he knew our meanings, could he scape?
ITHIMORE. No, none can heare him, cry he ne're so loud.
BARABAS. Why true, therefore did I place him there: 140
  The other Chambers open towards the street.
ITHIMORE. You loyter, master, wherefore stay we thus?
  Oh how I long to see him shake his heeles.

[2 FRYAR *is revealed.*]

124 requisite . . . not live] *Deighton*; not requisite . . . live *Q*

BARABAS. Come on, sirra, off with your girdle, make a
hansom noose; Fryar awake.   145

2 FRYAR. What doe you meane to strangle me?

ITHIMORE. Yes, 'cause you use to confesse.

BARABAS. Blame not us but the proverb, Confes and be
hang'd. Pull hard.

2 FRYAR. What will you have my life?   150

BARABAS. Pull hard, I say, you would have had my goods.

ITHIMORE. I, and our lives too, therefore pull amaine.

[2 FRYAR *falls*.]

'Tis neatly done, Sir, here's no print at all.

BARABAS. Then is it as it should be, take him up.

ITHIMORE. Nay, Master, be rul'd by me a little; so, let   155
him leane upon his staffe; excellent, he stands as if
he were begging of Bacon.

BARABAS. Who would not thinke but that this Fryar liv'd?
What time a night is't now, sweet *Ithimore*?

ITHIMORE. Towards one.   160

BARABAS. Then will not *Jacomo* be long from hence. [*Exeunt*.]

Enter 1 FRYAR.

1 FRYAR. This is the houre wherein I shall proceed;
Oh happy houre, wherein I shall convert
An Infidell, and bring his gold into our treasury.
But soft, is not this *Bernardine*? it is;   165
And understanding I should come this way,
Stands here a purpose, meaning me some wrong,
And intercept my going to the Jew;
Bernardine;
Wilt thou not speake? thou think'st I see thee not;   170
Away, I'de wish thee, and let me goe by:
No, wilt thou not? nay then I'le force my way;
And see, a staffe stands ready for the purpose:
As thou lik'st that, stop me another time. *Strike him, he fals*.

Enter BARABAS [*and* ITHIMORE].

BARABAS. Why how now *Jacomo*, what hast thou done?   175

1 FRYAR. Why stricken him that would have stroke at me.

150 have] *Chappell*; save *Q*

BARABAS. Who is it, *Bernardine?* now out alas, he is slaine.

ITHIMORE. I, Master, he's slain; look how his brains
    drop out on's nose.

1 FRYAR. Good sirs I have don't, but no body knowes it   180
    but you two, I may escape.

BARABAS. So might my man and I hang with you for company.

ITHIMORE. No, let us beare him to the Magistrates.

1 FRYAR. Good *Barabas* let me goe.

BARABAS. No, pardon me, the Law must have his course.   185
    I must be forc'd to give in evidence,
    That being importun'd by this *Bernardine*
    To be a Christian, I shut him out,
    And there he sate: now I to keepe my word,
    And give my goods and substance to your house,   190
    Was up thus early; with intent to goe
    Unto your Friery, because you staid.

ITHIMORE. Fie upon 'em, Master, will you turne
    Christian, when holy Friars turne devils and murder
    one another.
                                      195

BARABAS. No, for this example I'le remaine a Jew:
    Heaven blesse me; what, a Fryar a murderer?
    When shall you see a Jew commit the like?

ITHIMORE. Why a Turke could ha done no more.

BARABAS. To morrow is the Sessions; you shall to it.   200
    Come *Ithimore*, let's helpe to take him hence.

1 FRYAR. Villaines, I am a sacred person, touch me not.

BARABAS. The Law shall touch you, we'll but lead you, we:
    'Las I could weepe at your calamity.
    Take in the staffe too, for that must be showne: 205
    Law wils that each particular be knowne.   *Exeunt.*

[*Scaena* 2.]

Enter CURTEZANE, *and* PILIA-BORZA.

CURTEZANE. *Pilia-borza*, didst thou meet with *Ithimore*?

PILIA-BORZA. I did.

CURTEZANE. And didst thou deliver my letter?

PILIA-BORZA. I did.

CURTEZANE. And what think'st thou, will he come?   5

PILIA-BORZA. I think so, and yet I cannot tell, for at the
reading of the letter, he look'd like a man of another
world.

CURTEZANE. Why so?

PILIA-BORZA. That such a base slave as he should be   10
saluted by such a tall man as I am, from such a beautifull dame as you.

CURTEZANE. And what said he?

PILIA-BORZA. Not a wise word, only gave me a nod, as
who shold say, Is it even so; and so I left him, being   15
driven to a *Non-plus* at the critical aspect of my terri-
ble countenance.

CURTEZANE. And where didst meet him?

PILIA-BORZA. Upon mine owne free-hold, within fortie
foot of the gallowes, conning his neck-verse I take it,   20
looking of a Fryars Execution, whom I saluted with
an old hempen proverb, *Hodie tibi, cras mihi*, and so I
left him to the mercy of the Hangman: but the
Exercise being done, see where he comes.

Enter ITHIMORE.

ITHIMORE. I never knew a man take his death so   25
patiently as this Fryar; he was ready to leape off e're
the halter was about his necke; and when the
Hangman had put on his hempen Tippet, he made
such haste to his prayers, as if hee had had another
Cure to serve; well, goe whither he will, I'le be none   30
of his followers in haste: and now I thinke on't, going
to the execution, a fellow met me with a muschatoes
like a Ravens wing, and a Dagger with a hilt like a

warming-pan, and he gave me a letter from one
Madam *Bellamira*, saluting me in such sort as if he   35
had meant to make cleane my Boots with his lips; the
effect was, that I should come to her house; I wonder
what the reason is; it may be she sees more in me
than I can find in my selfe; for she writes further,
that she loves me ever since she saw me, and who   40
would not requite such love? here's her house, and
here she comes, and now would I were gone, I am
not worthy to looke upon her.

PILIA-BORZA. This is the Gentleman you writ to.

ITHIMORE. Gentleman, he flouts me, what gentry can be   45
in a poore Turke of ten pence? I'le be gone.

CURTEZANE. Is't not a sweet fac'd youth, *Pilia*?

ITHIMORE. Agen, sweet youth; did not you, Sir, bring
the sweet youth a letter?

PILIA-BORZA. I did Sir, and from this Gentlewoman,   50
who as my selfe, and the rest of the family, stand or
fall at your service.

CURTEZANE. Though womans modesty should hale me backe,
I can with-hold no longer; welcome sweet love.

ITHIMORE. Now am I cleane, or rather fouly out of the way. 55
                                                   [*Aside.*]

CURTEZANE. Whither so soone?

ITHIMORE. I'le goe steale some mony from my Master to
make me hansome: Pray pardon me, I must goe see a
ship discharg'd.   [*Aside.*]

CURTEZANE. Canst thou be so unkind to leave me thus?   60

PILIA-BORZA. And ye did but know how she loves you, Sir.

ITHIMORE. Nay, I care not how much she loves me;
sweet *Allamira*, would I had my Masters wealth for
thy sake.

PILIA-BORZA. And you can have it, Sir, and if you please. 65

ITHIMORE. If 'twere above ground I could, and would
have it; but hee hides and buries it up as Partridges
doe their egges, under the earth.

PILIA-BORZA. And is't not possible to find it out?

ITHIMORE. By no meanes possible.   70

CURTEZANE. What shall we doe with this base villaine then?
                                                   [*Aside.*]

PILIA-BORZA. Let me alone, doe but you speake him
    faire: [*Aside.*]
      But you know some secrets of the Jew, which if
    they were reveal'd, would doe him harme.
ITHIMORE. I, and such as—Goe to, no more, I'le make   75
    him send me half he has, and glad he scapes so too.
    Pen and Inke:
    I'le write unto him, we'le have mony strait.
PILIA-BORZA. Send for a hundred Crownes at least.   79
ITHIMORE. Ten hundred thousand crownes,   *He writes.*
    —Master *Barabas.*
PILIA-BORZA. Write not so submissively, but threatning him.
ITHIMORE. Sirra *Barabas*, send me a hundred crownes.
PILIA-BORZA. Put in two hundred at least.
ITHIMORE. I charge thee send me three hundred by this   85
    bearer, and this shall be your warrant; if you doe not,
    no more but so.
PILIA-BORZA. Tell him you will confesse.
ITHIMORE. Otherwise I'le confesse all; vanish and returne
    in a twinckle.   90
PILIA-BORZA. Let me alone, I'le use him in his kinde.   [*Exit.*]
ITHIMORE. Hang him Jew.
CURTEZANE. Now, gentle *Ithimore*, lye in my lap.
    Where are my Maids? provide a running Banquet;
    Send to the Merchant, bid him bring me silkes,   95
    Shall *Ithimore* my love goe in such rags?
ITHIMORE. And bid the Jeweller come hither too.
CURTEZANE. I have no husband, sweet, I'le marry thee.
ITHIMORE. Content, but we will leave this paltry land,
    And saile from hence to *Greece*, to lovely *Greece*,   100
    I'le be thy *Jason*, thou my golden Fleece;
    Where painted Carpets o're the meads are hurl'd,
    And *Bacchus* vineyards over-spread the world:
    Where Woods and Forrests goe in goodly greene,
    I'le be *Adonis*, thou shalt be Loves Queene.   105
    The Meads, the Orchards, and the Primrose lanes,
    Instead of Sedge and Reed, beare Sugar Canes:
    Thou in those Groves, by *Dis* above,
    Shalt live with me and be my love.
        102 over-spread] *Reed*; ore-spread *Q*

CURTEZANE. Whither will I not goe with gentle *Ithimore*?   110

Enter PILIA-BORZA.

ITHIMORE. How now? hast thou the gold?

PILIA-BORZA. Yes.

ITHIMORE. But came it freely, did the Cow give down her milk freely?

PILIA-BORZA. At reading of the letter, he star'd and   115
stamp'd, and turnd aside, I tooke him by the beard, and look'd upon him thus; told him he were best to send it, then he hug'd and imbrac'd me.

ITHIMORE. Rather for feare then love.

PILIA-BORZA. Then like a Jew he laugh'd and jeer'd,   120
and told me he lov'd me for your sake, and said what a faithfull servant you had bin.

ITHIMORE. The more villaine he to keep me thus: here's goodly 'parrell, is there not?

PILIA-BORZA. To conclude, he gave me ten crownes.   125

ITHIMORE. But ten? I'le not leave him worth a gray groat, give me a Reame of paper, we'll have a king-dome of gold for't.

PILIA-BORZA. Write for five hundred Crownes.

ITHIMORE. Sirra Jew, as you love your life send me five   130
hundred crowns, and give the Bearer one hundred. Tell him I must hav't.

PILIA-BORZA. I warrant your worship shall hav't.

ITHIMORE. And if he aske why I demand so much, tell him, I scorne to write a line under a hundred   135
crownes.

PILIA-BORZA. You'd make a rich Poet, Sir. I am gone.

Exit.

ITHIMORE. Take thou the mony, spend it for my sake.

CURTEZANE. 'Tis not thy mony, but thy selfe I weigh:
Thus *Bellamira* esteemes of gold;   [*Throw it aside.*]
But thus of thee. —*Kisse him.*

ITHIMORE. That kisse againe; she runs division of my   141
lips. What an eye she casts on me? It twinckles like a Starre.

CURTEZANE. Come my deare love, let's in and sleepe together.

ITHIMORE. Oh that ten thousand nights were put in one,   145
     That wee might sleepe seven yeeres together
     Afore we wake.
CURTEZANE. Come Amorous wag, first banquet and then
     sleepe.

[Exeunt.]

[*Scaena* 3.]

Enter BARABAS *reading a letter.*

BARABAS. *Barabas* send me three hundred Crownes.
Plaine *Barabas*: oh that wicked Curtezane!
He was not wont to call me *Barabas*.
Or else I will confesse: I, there it goes:
But if I get him, *Coupe de Gorge* for that.   5
He sent a shaggy totter'd staring slave,
That when he speakes, drawes out his grisly beard,
And winds it twice or thrice about his eare;
Whose face has bin a grind-stone for mens swords,
His hands are hackt, some fingers cut quite off;   10
Who when he speakes, grunts like a hog, and looks
Like one that is imploy'd in Catzerie,
And crosbiting; such a Rogue
As is the husband to a hundred whores:
And I by him must send three hundred crownes.   15
Well, my hope is, he will not stay there still;
And when he comes: Oh that he were but here!

Enter PILIA-BORZA.

PILIA-BORZA. Jew, I must ha more gold.
BARABAS. Why wantst thou any of thy tale?
PILIA-BORZA. No; but three hundred will not serve his   20
    turne.
BARABAS. Not serve his turne, Sir?
PILIA-BORZA. No Sir; and therefore I must have five
    hundred more.
BARABAS. I'le rather—   25
PILIA-BORZA. Oh good words, Sir, and send it you were
    best; see, there's his letter.
BARABAS. Might he not as well come as send; pray bid
    him come and fetch it, what hee writes for you, ye
    shall have streight.   30
PILIA-BORZA. I, and the rest too, or else—
BARABAS. I must make this villaine away; please you dine
    with me, Sir, and you shal be most hartily poyson'd. *aside.*

PILIA-BORZA. No god-a-mercy, shall I have these crownes?

BARABAS. I cannot doe it, I have lost my keyes.   35

PILIA-BORZA. Oh, if that be all, I can picke ope your locks.

BARABAS. Or climbe up to my Counting-house window:
    you know my meaning.

PILIA-BORZA. I know enough, and therfore talke not to
    me of your counting-house, the gold, or know Jew it   40
    is in my power to hang thee.

BARABAS. I am betraid.   [*Aside.*]
    'Tis not five hundred Crownes that I esteeme,
    I am not mov'd at that: this angers me,
    That he who knowes I love him as my self   45
    Should write in this imperious vaine? why Sir,
    You know I have no childe, and unto whom
    Should I leave all but unto *Ithimore*?

PILIA-BORZA. Here's many words but no crownes; the
    crownes.

BARABAS. Commend me to him, Sir, most humbly,   50
    And unto your good mistris as unknowne.

PILIA-BORZA. Speake, shall I have 'um, Sir?

BARABAS. Sir, here they are.
    Oh that I should part with so much gold!   [*Aside.*]
    Here take 'em, fellow, with as good a will—   55
    —As I wud see thee hang'd;   [*Aside.*]
                  oh, love stops my breath:
    Never lov'd man servant as I doe *Ithimore*.

PILIA-BORZA. I know it, Sir.

BARABAS. Pray when, Sir, shall I see you at my house?

PILIA-BORZA. Soone enough to your cost, Sir: Fare you
    well.   *Exit.*

BARABAS. Nay to thine owne cost, villaine, if thou com'st.   61
    Was ever Jew tormented as I am?
    To have a shag-rag knave to come demand
    Three hundred Crownes, and then five hundred Crownes?
    Well, I must seeke a meanes to rid 'em all,   65
    And presently: for in his villany
    He will tell all he knowes and I shall dye for't.
    I have it.

63 demand] *add. Bowers*

I will in some disguize goe see the slave,
And how the villaine revels with my gold.   *Exit.*

[*Scaena* 4.]

Enter CURTEZANE, ITHIMORE, PILIA-BORZA.

CURTEZANE. I'le pledge thee, love, and therefore drinke
it off.

ITHIMORE. Saist thou me so? have at it; and doe you heare?
[*Whispers to her.*]

CURTEZANE. Goe to, it shall be so.

ITHIMORE. Of that condition I wil drink it up; here's to thee.

CURTEZANE. Nay, I'le have all or none.   6

ITHIMORE. There, if thou lov'st me doe not leave a drop.

CURTEZANE. Love thee, fill me three glasses.

ITHIMORE. Three and fifty dozen, I'le pledge thee.

PILIA-BORZA. Knavely spoke, and like a Knight at 10
Armes.

ITHIMORE. Hey *Rivo Castiliano*, a man's a man.

CURTEZANE. Now to the Jew.

ITHIMORE. Ha to the Jew, and send me mony you were best.

PILIA-BORZA. What wudst thou doe if he should send 15
thee none?

ITHIMORE. Doe nothing; but I know what I know, He's
a murderer.

CURTEZANE. I had not thought he had been so brave a man.

ITHIMORE. You knew *Mathias* and the Governors son, 20
he and I kild 'em both, and yet never touch'd 'em.

PILIA-BORZA. Oh bravely done.

ITHIMORE. I carried the broth that poyson'd the Nuns,
and he and I snicle hand too fast, strangled a Fryar.

CURTEZANE. You two alone?   25

ITHIMORE. We two, and 'twas never knowne, nor never
shall be for me.

PILIA-BORZA. This shall with me unto the Governor. [*aside.*]

CURTEZANE. And fit it should: but first let's ha more gold:
[*aside.*]

Come gentle *Ithimore*, lye in my lap.   30

ITHIMORE. Love me little, love me long, let musicke rumble,
Whilst I in thine incony lap doe tumble.

Enter BARABAS *with a Lute, disguis'd.*

CURTEZANE. A French Musician, come let's heare your skill?

BARABAS. Must tuna my Lute for sound, twang twang first.

ITHIMORE. Wilt drinke French-man, here's to thee with   35
a—pox on this drunken hick-up.

BARABAS. Gramercy Mounsier.

CURTEZANE. Prethe, *Pilia-borza*, bid the Fidler give me
the posey in his hat there.

PILIA-BORZA. Sirra, you must give my mistris your posey.   40

BARABAS. *A voustre commandemente Madam.*

CURTEZANE. How sweet, my *Ithimore*, the flowers smell.

ITHIMORE. Like thy breath, sweet-hart, no violet like 'em.

PILIA-BORZA. Foh, me thinkes they stinke like a Holly-
Hoke.   45

BARABAS. So, now I am reveng'd upon 'em all.   [*aside.*]
The scent thereof was death, I poyson'd it.

ITHIMORE. Play, Fidler, or I'le cut your cats guts into
chitterlins.

BARABAS. Pardona moy, be no in tune yet; so now, now   50
all be in.

ITHIMORE. Give him a crowne, and fill me out more wine.

PILIA-BORZA. There's two crownes for thee, play.

BARABAS. How liberally the villain gives me mine own gold.
        aside.

PILIA-BORZA. Me thinke he fingers very well.   55

BARABAS. So did you when you stole my gold.   *aside.*

PILIA-BORZA. How swift he runnes.

BARABAS. You run swifter when you threw my gold out
of my Window.   *aside.*

CURTEZANE. Musician, hast beene in *Malta* long?   60

BARABAS. Two, three, foure month Madam.

ITHIMORE. Dost not know a Jew, one *Barabas*?

BARABAS. Very mush, Mounsier, you no be his man?

PILIA-BORZA. His man?

ITHIMORE. I scorne the Peasant, tell him so.   65

BARABAS. He knowes it already.   [*aside.*]

ITHIMORE. 'Tis a strange thing of that Jew, he lives
upon pickled Grashoppers, and sauc'd Mushrumbs.

BARABAS. What a slave's this? The Governour feeds not

as I doe.   *aside.*

ITHIMORE. He never put on cleane shirt since he was   71
   circumcis'd.

BARABAS. Oh raskall! I change my selfe twice a day.   *aside.*

ITHIMORE. The Hat he weares, *Judas* left under the
   Elder when he hang'd himselfe.   75

BARABAS. 'Twas sent me for a present from the great *Cham.*
                                            aside.

PILIA-BORZA. A masty slave he is; whether now, Fidler?

BARABAS. Pardona moy, Mounsier, me be no well.   *Exit.*

PILIA-BORZA. Farewel Fidler: One letter more to the Jew.

CURTEZANE. Prethe sweet love, one more, and write it   80
   sharp.

ITHIMORE. No, I'le send by word of mouth now; bid
   him deliver thee a thousand Crownes, by the same
   token, that the Nuns lov'd Rice, that Fryar
   Bernardine slept in his owne clothes, any of 'em will   85
   doe it.

PILIA-BORZA. Let me alone to urge it now I know the
   meaning.

ITHIMORE. The meaning has a meaning; come let's in:
  To undoe a Jew is charity, and not sinne.   90
                                        Exeunt.

Actus Quintus [Scaena 1].

Enter GOVERNOR, KNIGHTS, MARTIN DEL BOSCO
[*and* OFFICERS].

GOVERNOR. Now, Gentlemen, betake you to your Armes,
And see that *Malta* be well fortifi'd;
And it behoves you to be resolute;
For *Calymath* having hover'd here so long,
Will winne the Towne, or dye before the wals.   5
1 KNIGHT. And dye he shall, for we will never yeeld.

Enter CURTEZANE, PILIA-BORZA.

CURTEZANE. Oh bring us to the Governor.
GOVERNOR. Away with her, she is a Curtezane.
CURTEZANE. What e're I am, yet Governor heare me speake;
I bring thee newes by whom thy sonne was slaine: 10
Mathias did it not, it was the Jew.
PILIA-BORZA. Who, besides the slaughter of these
Gentlemen, poyson'd his owne daughter and the
Nuns, strangled a Fryar, and I know not what mis-
chiefe beside.   15
GOVERNOR. Had we but proofe of this.
CURTEZANE. Strong proofe, my Lord, his man's now at
my lodging that was his Agent, he'll confesse it all.
GOVERNOR. Goe fetch him straight.   [*Exeunt* OFFICERS.]
I always fear'd that Jew.

Enter BARABAS, ITHIMORE [*with* OFFICERS].

BARABAS. I'le goe alone, dogs, do not hale me thus.   20
ITHIMORE. Nor me neither, I cannot out-run you
Constable, oh my belly.
BARABAS. One dram of powder more had made all sure.
What a damn'd slave was I?   [*Aside.*]
GOVERNOR. Make fires, heat irons, let the racke be fetch'd.   25
1 KNIGHT. Nay stay, my Lord, 'tmay be he will confesse.
BARABAS. Confesse; what meane you, Lords, who should
confesse?
GOVERNOR. Thou and thy Turk; 'twas you that slew my son.

ITHIMORE. Gilty, my Lord, I confesse; your sonne and   30
    Mathias were both contracted unto *Abigall*, he
    forg'd a counterfeit challenge.
BARABAS. Who carried that challenge?
ITHIMORE. I carried it, I confesse, but who writ it?
    Marry, even he that strangled *Bernardine*, poyson'd   35
    the Nuns, and his owne daughter.
GOVERNOR. Away with him, his sight is death to me.
BARABAS. For what? you men of *Malta*, heare me speake;
    Shee is a Curtezane and he a theefe,
    And he my bondman, let me have law,   40
    For none of this can prejudice my life:
GOVERNOR. Once more away with him; you shall have law.
BARABAS. Devils doe your worst, I'le live in spite of you.
    As these have spoke so be it to their soules:
    I hope the poyson'd flowers will worke anon.   [*Aside.*]
            Exeunt [BARABAS, ITHIMORE, CURTEZANE,
                 PILIA-BORZA, OFFICERS].

Enter MATER.

MATER. Was my *Mathias* murder'd by the Jew?   46
    Ferneze, 'twas thy sonne that murder'd him.
GOVERNOR. Be patient, gentle Madam, it was he,
    He forged the daring challenge made them fight.
MATER. Where is the Jew, where is that murderer?   50
GOVERNOR. In prison till the Law has past on him.

Enter OFFICER.

OFFICER. My Lord, the Curtezane and her man are dead;
    So is the Turke, and *Barabas* the Jew.
GOVERNOR. Dead?
OFFICER. Dead, my Lord, and here they bring his body.   55

    [*Enter* OFFICERS *carrying* BARABAS *as dead.*]

BOSCO. This sudden death of his is very strange.
GOVERNOR. Wonder not at it, Sir, the heavens are just:
    Their deaths were like their lives, then think not of 'em;
    Since they are dead, let them be buried.
    For the Jewes body, throw that o're the wals,   60

        31 he] *add. Reed*   43 I'le] *Dyce*; I *Q*

To be a prey for Vultures and wild beasts.
So, now away and fortifie the Towne.

Exeunt [*Manet* BARABAS].

BARABAS. What, all alone? well fare sleepy drinke.
I'le be reveng'd on this accursed Towne;
For by my meanes *Calymath* shall enter in.   65
I'le helpe to slay their children and their wives,
To fire the Churches, pull their houses downe,
Take my goods too, and seize upon my lands:
I hope to see the Governour a slave,
And, rowing in a Gally, whipt to death.   70

Enter CALYMATH, BASSOES, TURKES.

CALYMATH. Whom have we there, a spy?
BARABAS. Yes, my good Lord, one that can spy a place
Where you may enter, and surprize the Towne:
My name is *Barabas*; I am a Jew.
CALYMATH. Art thou that Jew whose goods we heard were sold
For Tribute-mony?
BARABAS.   The very same, my Lord: 76
And since that time they have hir'd a slave my man
To accuse me of a thousand villanies:
I was imprison'd, but escap'd their hands.
CALYMATH. Didst breake prison?   80
BARABAS. No, no:
I dranke of Poppy and cold mandrake juyce;
And being asleepe, belike they thought me dead,
And threw me o're the wals: so, or how else,
The Jew is here, and rests at your command.   85
CALYMATH. 'Twas bravely done: but tell me, *Barabas*,
Canst thou, as thou reportest, make *Malta* ours?
BARABAS. Feare not, my Lord, for here against the Sluice,
The rocke is hollow, and of purpose digg'd,
To make a passage for the running streames   90
And common channels of the City.
Now whilst you give assault unto the wals,
I'le lead five hundred souldiers through the Vault,
And rise with them i'th middle of the Towne,

79 escap'd] *Scott*; scap'd *Q*   88 Sluice] *Broughton*; Truce *Q*

Open the gates for you to enter in,   95
And by this means the City is your owne.
CALYMATH. If this be true, I'le make thee Governor.
BARABAS. And if it be not true, then let me dye.
CALYMATH. Thou'st doom'd thy selfe, assault it presently.

Exeunt.

[*Scaena* 2.]

Alarmes. Enter [CALYMATH *and*] Turkes, BARABAS,
    GOVERNOR, *and* Knights *prisoners.*

CALYMATH. Now vaile your pride you captive Christians,
  And kneele for mercy to your conquering foe:
  Now where's the hope you had of haughty *Spaine?*
  Ferneze, speake, had it not beene much better
  To keep thy promise then be thus surpriz'd?   5
GOVERNOR. What should I say, we are captives and
  must yeeld.
CALYMATH. I, villains, you must yeeld, and under
  Turkish yokes
  Shall groning beare the burthen of our ire;
  And *Barabas*, as erst we promis'd thee,
  For thy desert we make thee Governor,   10
  Use them at thy discretion.
BARABAS.   Thankes, my Lord.
GOVERNOR. Oh fatall day, to fall into the hands
  Of such a Traitor and unhallowed Jew!
  What greater misery could heaven inflict?
CALYMATH. 'Tis our command: and *Barabas*, we give   15
  To guard thy person, these our Janizaries:
  Intreate them well, as we have used thee.
  And now, brave Bashawes, come, wee'll walke about
  The ruin'd Towne, and see the wracke we made:
  Farewell brave Jew, farewell great *Barabas*.   20
                  Exeunt [CALYMATH *and* Turkes].
BARABAS. May all good fortune follow *Calymath*.
  And now, as entrance to our safety,
  To prison with the Governour and these
  Captives, his consorts and confederates.
GOVERNOR. Oh villaine, Heaven will be reveng'd on thee. 25
BARABAS. Away, no more, let him not trouble me.
               Exeunt [GOVERNOR *and* Knights].
  Thus hast thou gotten, by thy policie,

---

3 *after* 10 *Q*   5 keep] *Wagner*; kept *Q*   10 thee] *Reed*; the *Q*
24 Captives] Captaines *Q*

No simple place, no small authority,
I am now Governour of *Malta*; true,
But *Malta* hates me, and in hating me   30
My life's in danger, and what boots it thee
Poore *Barabas*, to be the Governour,
When as thy life shall be at their command?
No, *Barabas*, this must be look'd into;
And since by wrong thou got'st Authority,   35
Maintaine it bravely by firme policy,
At least unprofitably lose it not:
For he that liveth in Authority,
And neither gets him friends, nor fils his bags,
Lives like the Asse that *Aesope* speaketh of,   40
That labours with a load of bread and wine,
And leaves it off to snap on Thistle tops:
But *Barabas* will be more circumspect.
Begin betimes, Occasion's bald behind,
Slip not thine oportunity, for feare too late   45
Thou seek'st for much, but canst not compasse it.
Within here.

Enter GOVERNOR *with a* Guard.

GOVERNOR.   My Lord?
BARABAS.   I, Lord, thus slaves will learne.
Now Governor—stand by there, wait within;   [*Exit* Guard.]
This is the reason that I sent for thee;
Thou seest thy life, and *Malta's* happinesse,   50
Are at my Arbitrament; and *Barabas*
At his discretion may dispose of both:
Now tell me, Governor, and plainely too,
What think'st thou shall become of it and thee?
GOVERNOR. This; *Barabas*, since things are in thy power,   55
I see no reason but of *Malta's* wracke,
Nor hope of thee but extreme cruelty,
Nor feare I death, nor will I flatter thee.
BARABAS. Governor, good words, be not so furious;
'Tis not thy life which can availe me ought,   60
Yet you doe live, and live for me you shall:
And as for *Malta's* ruine, thinke you not
'Twere slender policy for *Barabas*

To dispossesse himselfe of such a place?
For sith, as once you said, within this Ile   65
In *Malta* here, that I have got my goods,
And in this City still have had successe,
And now at length am growne your Governor,
Your selves shall see it shall not be forgot:
For as a friend not knowne, but in distresse,   70
I'le reare up *Malta* now remedilesse.
GOVERNOR. Will *Barabas* recover *Malta's* losse?
Will *Barabas* be good to Christians?
BARABAS. What wilt thou give me, Governor, to procure
A dissolution of the slavish Bands   75
Wherein the Turke hath yoak'd your land and you?
What will you give me if I render you
The life of *Calymath*, surprize his men,
And in an out-house of the City shut
His souldiers, till I have consum'd 'em all with fire?   80
What will you give him that procureth this?
GOVERNOR. Doe but bring this to passe which thou pretendest,
Deale truly with us as thou intimatest,
And I will send amongst the Citizens
And by my letters privately procure   85
Great summes of mony for thy recompence:
Nay more, doe this, and live thou Governor still.
BARABAS. Nay, doe thou this, *Ferneze*, and be free;
Governor, I enlarge thee, live with me,
Goe walke about the City, see thy friends: 90
Tush, send not letters to 'em, goe thy selfe,
And let me see what mony thou canst make;
Here is my hand that I'le set *Malta* free:
And thus we cast it: To a solemne feast
I will invite young *Selim-Calymath*,   95
Where be thou present onely to performe
One stratagem that I'le impart to thee,
Wherein no danger shall betide thy life,
And I will warrant *Malta* free for ever.
GOVERNOR. Here is my hand, beleeve me, *Barabas*,   100
I will be there, and doe as thou desirest;
When is the time?
BARABAS.   Governor, presently.

For *Callymath*, when he hath view'd the Towne,
Will take his leave and saile towards *Ottoman*.
GOVERNOR. Then will I, *Barabas*, about this coyne,   105
And bring it with me to thee in the evening.
BARABAS. Doe so, but faile not; now farewell *Ferneze*:
                                        [*Exit* GOVERNOR.]
And thus farre roundly goes the businesse:
Thus loving neither, will I live with both,
Making a profit of my policie;   110
And he from whom my most advantage comes,
Shall be my friend.
This is the life we Jewes are us'd to lead;
And reason too, for Christians doe the like:
Well, now about effecting this device: 115
First to surprize great *Selims* souldiers,
And then to make provision for the feast,
That at one instant all things may be done,
My policie detests prevention:
To what event my secret purpose drives,   120
I know; and they shall witnesse with their lives.   *Exit.*

[*Scaena* 3.]

Enter CALYMATH, BASSOES.

CALYMATH. Thus have we view'd the City, seene the sacke,
And caus'd the ruines to be new repair'd,
Two lofty Turrets that command the Towne,
Which with our Bombards shot and Basiliske,
We rent in sunder at our entry: 5
And now I see the Scituation,
And how secure this conquer'd Iland stands
Inviron'd with the *Mediterranean* Sea,
Strong contermur'd with other petty Iles;
And toward *Calabria* back'd by *Sicily*,   10
Where *Siracusian Dionisius* reign'd;
I wonder how it could be conquer'd thus?

Enter a MESSENGER.

MESSENGER. From *Barabas*, *Malta's* Governor, I bring
A message unto mighty *Calymath*;
Hearing his Soveraigne was bound for Sea,   15
To saile to *Turkey*, to great *Ottoman*,
He humbly would intreat your Majesty
To come and see his homely Citadell,
And banquet with him e're thou leav'st the Ile.
CALYMATH. To banquet with him in his Citadell,   20
I feare me, Messenger, to feast my traine
Within a Towne of warre so lately pillag'd
Will be too costly and too troublesome:
Yet would I gladly visit *Barabas*,
For well has *Barabas* deserv'd of us.   25
MESSENGER. *Selim*, for that, thus saith the Governor,
That he hath in store a Pearle so big,
So precious, and withall so orient,
As be it valued but indifferently,
The price thereof will serve to entertaine   30
Selim and all his souldiers for a month;

---

3 *after 10 Q*   9 contermur'd] *conj. Collier, Deighton*; contermin'd *Q*   11 Where]
Robinson; When *Q*

Therefore he humbly would intreat your Highnesse
Not to depart till he has feasted you.
CALYMATH. I cannot feast my men in *Malta* wals,
Except he place his Tables in the streets.   35
MESSENGER. Know, *Selim*, that there is a monastery
Which standeth as an out-house to the Towne;
There will he banquet them, but thee at home,
With all thy Bashawes and brave followers.
CALYMATH. Well, tell the Governor we grant his suit,   40
Wee'll in this Summer Evening feast with him.
MESSENGER. I shall, my Lord.   *Exit.*
CALYMATH. And now bold Bashawes, let us to our Tents,
And meditate how we may grace us best
To solemnize our Governors great feast.   45
                                              Exeunt.

[*Scaena* 4.]

Enter GOVERNOR, KNIGHTS, DEL-BOSCO.

GOVERNOR. In this, my Countrimen, be rul'd by me,
   Have speciall care that no man sally forth
   Till you shall heare a Culverin discharg'd
   By him that beares the Linstocke, kindled thus;
   Then issue out and come to rescue me,   5
   For happily I shall be in distresse,
   Or you released of this servitude.
I KNIGHT. Rather then thus to live as Turkish thrals,
   What will we not adventure?
GOVERNOR. On then, begone.
KNIGHTS.   Farewell grave Governor.   10
                                        [*Exeunt.*]

[*Scaena* 5.]

Enter [BARABAS] *with a Hammar above, very busie*
[*, and* CARPENTERS].

BARABAS. How stand the cords? How hang these hinges, fast?
Are all the Cranes and Pulleyes sure?
CARPENTER.   All fast.
BARABAS. Leave nothing loose, all leveld to my mind.
Why now I see that you have Art indeed.
There, Carpenters, divide that gold amongst you: 5
Goe swill in bowles of Sacke and Muscadine:
Downe to the Celler, taste of all my wines.
CARPENTER. We shall, my Lord, and thanke you: *Exeunt*.
BARABAS. And if you like them, drinke your fill—and dye:
For so I live, perish may all the world.   10
Now *Selim-Calymath* returne me word
That thou wilt come, and I am satisfied.

Enter Messenger.

Now sirra, what, will he come?
MESSENGER. He will; and has commanded all his men
To come ashore, and march through *Malta* streets,   15
That thou maist feast them in thy Citadell.   [*Exit* Messenger.]
BARABAS. Then now are all things as my wish wud have 'em,
There wanteth nothing but the Governors pelfe,
And see he brings it:

Enter GOVERNOR.

Now, Governor, the summe.
GOVERNOR. With free consent a hundred thousand pounds.   20
BARABAS. Pounds saist thou, Governor, wel since it is no more
I'le satisfie my selfe with that; nay, keepe it still,
For if I keepe not promise, trust not me.
And Governour, now partake my policy:
First for his Army they are sent before,   25
Enter'd the Monastery, and underneath
In severall places are field-pieces pitch'd,

2 CARPENTER] *Serv* Q

Bombards, whole Barrels full of Gunpowder,
That on the sudden shall dissever it,
And batter all the stones about their eares, 30
Whence none can possibly escape alive:
Now as for *Calymath* and his consorts,
Here have I made a dainty Gallery,
The floore whereof, this Cable being cut,
Doth fall asunder; so that it doth sinke 35
Into a deepe pit past recovery.
Here, hold that knife, and when thou seest he comes,
And with his Bashawes shall be blithely set,
A warning-peece shall be shot off from the Tower,
To give thee knowledge when to cut the cord, 40
And fire the house; say, will not this be brave?

GOVERNOR. Oh excellent! here, hold thee, *Barabas*,
I trust thy word, take what I promis'd thee.

BARABAS. No, Governor, I'le satisfie thee first,
Thou shalt not live in doubt of any thing. 45
Stand close, for here they come:

                [GOVERNOR *retires.*]
             why, is not this
A kingly kinde of trade to purchase Townes
By treachery, and sell 'em by deceit?
Now tell me, worldlings, underneath the sunne,
If greater falshood ever has bin done. 50

         Enter CALYMATH *and* BASSOES.

CALYMATH. Come, my Companion-Bashawes, see I pray
How busie *Barrabas* is there above
To entertaine us in his Gallery;
Let us salute him, Save thee, *Barabas*.

BARABAS. Welcome great *Calymath*. 55

GOVERNOR. How the slave jeeres at him?

BARABAS. Will't please thee, mighty *Selim-Calymath*,
To ascend our homely stayres?

CALYMATH.   I, *Barabas*,
Come Bashawes, attend.

GOVERNOR [*comes forward*] Stay, *Calymath*;

          49 sunne] *Reed*; summe *Q*

For I will shew thee greater curtesie   60
Then *Barabas* would have affoorded thee.
1 KNIGHT. Sound a charge there.
      A charge [within], the cable cut. A Caldron discovered
            [and BARABAS *falls into it].*

      [*Enter* DEL BOSCO *and* Knights.]

CALYMATH. How now, what means this?
BARABAS. Helpe, helpe me, Christians, helpe.
GOVERNOR. See *Calymath*, this was devis'd for thee.   65
CALYMATH. Treason, treason, Bashawes flye.
GOVERNOR. No, *Selim*, doe not flye;
  See his end first, and flye then if thou canst:
BARABAS. Oh helpe me, *Selim*, helpe me, Christians.
  Governour, why stand you all so pittilesse?   70
GOVERNOR. Should I in pitty of thy plaints or thee,
  Accursed *Barabas*; base Jew, relent:
  No, thus I'le see thy treachery repaid,
  But wish thou hadst behav'd thee otherwise.
BARABAS. You will not helpe me then?
GOVERNOR.   No, villaine, no.   75
BARABAS. And villaines, know you cannot helpe me now.
  Then *Barabas* breathe forth thy latest fate,
  And in the fury of thy torments, strive
  To end thy life with resolution:
  Know, Governor, 'twas I that slewe thy sonne;   80
  I fram'd the challenge that did make them meet:
  Know, *Calymath*, I aym'd thy overthrow,
  And had I but escap'd this strategem,
  I would have brought confusion on you all,
  Damn'd Christian dogges, and Turkish Infidels;   85
  But not begins the extremity of heat
  To pinch me with intolerable pangs:
  Dye life, flye soule, tongue curse thy fill and dye.   [*Dies.*]
CALYMATH. Tell me, you Christians, what doth this portend?
GOVERNOR. This traine he laid to have intrap'd thy life;   90
  Now *Selim* note the unhallowed deeds of Jewes:
  Thus he determin'd to have handled thee,
  But I have rather chose to save thy life.

      85 Christian] *Broughton*; Christians, *Q*

CALYMATH. Was this the banquet he prepar'd for us?
Let's hence, lest further mischiefe be pretended.   95
GOVERNOR. Nay, *Selim*, stay, for since we have thee here,
We will not let thee part so suddenly:
Besides, if we should let thee goe, all's one,
For with thy Gallyes couldst thou not get hence,
Without fresh men to rigge and furnish them.   100
CALYMATH. Tush, Governor, take thou no care for that,
My men are all aboord,
And doe attend my comming there by this.
GOVERNOUR. Why heardst thou not the trumpet sound a
charge?
CALYMATH. Yes, what of that?
GOVERNOR.   Why then the house was fir'd,
Blowne up and all thy souldiers massacred.   106
CALYMATH. Oh monstrous treason!
GOVERNOR.   A Jewes curtesie:
For he that did by treason worke our fall,
By treason hath delivered thee to us:
Know therefore, till thy father hath made good   110
The ruines done to *Malta* and to us,
Thou canst not part: for *Malta* shall be freed,
Or *Selim* ne're return to *Ottoman*.
CALYMATH. Nay rather, Christians, let me goe to *Turkey*,
In person there to mediate your peace;   115
To keepe me here will nought advantage you.
GOVERNOR. Content thee, *Calymath*, here thou must stay,
And live in *Malta* prisoner; for come all the world
To rescue thee, so will we guard us now,
As sooner shall they drinke the Ocean dry,   120
Then conquer *Malta*, or endanger us.
So march away, and let due praise be given
Neither to Fate nor Fortune, but to Heaven.   [*Exeunt.*]

FINIS

115 mediate] *Chappell*; meditate *Q*   118 all] *Reed*; call Q

APPENDIX

TO
MY WORTHY FRIEND,
M^r. THOMAS HAMMON,
OF GRAYES INNE, &c.

This Play, composed by so worthy an Authour as Mr.
Marlo; and the part of the Jew presented by so unimitable
an Actor as Mr. *Allin*, being in this later Age commended
to the Stage: As I usher'd it unto the Court, and presented it to the Cock-pit, with these Prologues and   5
Epilogues here inserted, so now being newly brought to
the Presse, I was loath it should be published without the
ornament of an Epistle; making choyce of you unto whom
to devote it; then whom (of all those Gentlemen and
acquaintance, within the compasse of my long knowledge) 10
there is none more able to taxe Ignorance, or attribute
right to merit. Sir, you have bin pleased to grace some of
mine owne workes with your curteous patronage; I hope
this will not be the worse accepted, because commended
by mee; over whom none can clayme more power or priv-   15
ilege than your selfe. I had no better a New-yeares gift to
present you with; receive it therefore as a continuance of
that inviolable obliegement, by which, he rests still
ingaged; who as he ever hath, shall alwayes remaine,

Tuissimus:
Tho. Heywood.

The Prologue spoken at Court.

Gracious and Great, that we so boldly dare,
('Mongst other Playes that now in fashion are)

To present this; writ many yeares agone,
And in that Age, thought second unto none;
We humbly crave your pardon: we pursue 5
The story of a rich and famous *Jew*
Who liv'd in *Malta*: you shall find him still,
In all his projects, a sound *Machevill*;
And that's his Character: He that hath past
So many Censures, is now come at last 10
To have your princely Eares, grace you him; then
You crowne the Action, and renowne the pen.

Epilogue.

It is our feare (dread Soveraigne) we have bin
Too tedious; neither can 't be lesse than sinne
To wrong your Princely patience: If we have,
(Thus low dejected) we your pardon crave:
And if ought here offend your eare or sight, 5
We onely Act, and Speake, what others write.

The Prologue to the Stage, at the Cocke-pit.

We know not how our play may passe this Stage,
But by the best of *Poets in that age   *Marlo.
The *Malta Jew* had being, and was made;
And He, then, by the best of *Actors play'd: *Allin.
In *Hero and Leander*, one did gaine 5
A lasting memorie: in *Tamberlaine*,
This *Jew*, with others many: th'other wan
The Attribute of peerelesse, being a man
Whom we may ranke with (doing no one wrong)
Proteus for shapes, and *Roscius* for a tongue, 10
So could he speake, so vary; nor is't hate
To merit in *him who doth personate   *Perkins.
Our *Jew* this day, nor is it his ambition
To exceed, or equall, being of condition

More modest; this is all that he intends,   15
(And that too, at the urgence of some friends)
To prove his best, and if none here gaine-say it,
The part he hath studied, and intends to play it.

Epilogue.

In Graving, with *Pigmalion* to contend;
Or painting, with *Apelles*; doubtlesse the end
Must be disgrace: our Actor did not so,
He onely aym'd to goe, but not out-goe.
Nor thinke that this day any prize was plaid,   5
Here were no betts at all, no wagers laid;
All the ambition that his mind doth swell
Is but to heare from you, (by me) 'twas well.

ACCIDENTAL EMENDATIONS

PROLOGUE
    12 off,] ~;   19 Empery] Empire   21 *Dracos] Drancus*   29 *Britanie] Britaine*

ACT I SCENE i
    1 BARABAS] *Jew (and throughout this scene)*   2 Persian] *Persian*   4 Samnites]
Samintes   5 Spanish] *Spanish*   6 silverlings] silverbings   19 Indian]
Indian   21 Moore] *Moore* Easterne] *Easterne*   23 stones,] ~;   24 weight;] ~,
25–7 Opals, Saphires, Amatists, Jacints . . . Topas . . . Emeraulds Rubyes . . .
Diamonds] *Opals, Saphires, Amatists, Jacints . . . Topas . . . Emeraulds . . . Rubyes . . .
Diamonds*   39 Halcions] *Halcions*   40 East] *East*   41 East] *East* South] *South*
47 *Mediterranean*] Mediterranean   48 1 MERCHANT] *Merch (and throughout the scene)*
66 amongst] amougst   71 *Caire*] Caire   79 Tush,] ~; wise;] ~,   84 Rhode,] ~.
86 Persian] *Persian*   95 Turke] *Turke*   101 every] enery   137 1 JEW] *prefixes for*
Jews *are* 1, 2, 3 me,] ~ₐ   156 Turkes] *Turkes*   173 *Temanite] Temainte*
175 together] togethre   177 Turke] *Turke*   179 Turkes] *Turkes*   186 *proximus*]
proximas

ACT I SCENE ii
    0SD GOVERNOR] *Governors*   2 Malta] Malta Rhodes,] *Rhodes*:   4 *Mediterranean*]
Mediterranean   10, 17, 27, 32 Governour] Governours   35 day?] ~.
38 Hebrews] *Hebrwes*   42 then,] ~ₐ   43 Then,] ~ₐ   57 1 JEW] *Jew*
68 Turkes] *Turkes*   69 Jewes] *Jewes*   79 Hebrews] *Hebrews*   91 *dio*] deo
110 'Tis] ₐ~   111 What,] ~?   128 Governor] Governors   148 misery.] ~,
154 th'devils] ~ₐ~   156 Turke] *Turke*   159 *Exeunt*.] ~,   164 *Primus] Primas*
214 slaves] ssaves   223 day.] ~ₐ   244 Portagues] *Portagues*   299 seene,] ~.
304 'Tis thirtie] Tis 30   312 thou,] ~ₐ   329 lye.] ~,   344 thus † that] ~ₐ~
350 The . . . it] *italic*   353 Goe . . . not] *italic*   355 To morrow . . .
doore] *italic*   355 I'le] *Il'e*   358 Farewell . . . morning] *italic*

ACT I SCENE iii
    14 fourteene] 14

ACT II SCENE i
    39 *Bien . . . es*] *Birn para todos, my ga nada no er*   41 East] *East*   45 SD
bags.] ~, 50 Oh *Abigal*] ~ *Aigal*   63 Hermoso . . . Dineros] *Hermoso Piarer, de les
Denirch*   63SD *Exit*] *Exeunt*

ACT II SCENE ii
    9 Grecians, Turks, and Africk Moores] *Grecians, Turks,* and *Africk Moores*
21 Turkes] *Turkes*   25 Turke] *Turke*   28 Turkes] *Turkes*   33 Turkes.] *Turkes* ₐ
42, 46 Turkes] *Turkes*   56SD *Exeunt*] *Extunt*

ACT II SCENE iii
    4 *Q adds* SD *Ent. Bar. Q*   22 and] aud   46 Gentiles] *Gentiles*   98 two
hundred] 200   103 three hundred] 300   108 Moore] *Moore* two hundred] 200
110 Turke] *Turke* Moore] *Moore*   112 stone] stoue   114 SLAVE] *Itha.*
116, 119, 123 SLAVE] *Ith.*   139 SD MATHIAS.] ~.   183 Italian] *Italian*
184 enrich'd] enric'd   204 villages] villagss   231 *Abraham*] italic within italic aside *Q*
249 Manna] *Manna* Jewes] *Jewes*   297 yet] yer   302 Jebusite] *Jebusite*
303 Passeover] *Passeover*   326 Hebrewes] *Hebrewes*   331 rather] rathe

ACT III SCENE i
6 *Padua* ₔ] ~,   25 Zoons] Zoon's

ACT III SCENE ii
3–4 LODOWICKE . . . MATHIAS] *Math. . . . Lod.*   16 wounds.] woūds ₔ   17 grieve]
grive   25 Madam] Madem

ACT III SCENE iii
11 had.] ~ₔ   17 *Mathias* and Don *Lodowickes*] *Mathia* & Don *Lodowick*   21 Master]
Mʳ.   22 *Mathias*] *Mathia*   28 and] &   32 *Jaques*] Iaynes   38 gon.] ~ₔ
63 and] &   72 *Jacomo*] *Jacomi*

ACT III SCENE iv
45 halfe] helfe   51 *Exit.*] ~:   67 and plump] & ~   71 Italian] *Italian*
78 *Jaques*] *Jagues*   83 them.] ~,   88, 91 Master] Mʳ.   102 *Lerna's*]
Lerna's   103 Hebon] *Hebon*

ACT III SCENE v
OSD BASSO] *Bashaw*   1 Bashaw] *Bashaws*   3, 7 BASSO] *Bash.*   11 Bashaw]
Bashaw   19 BASSO] *Bash.*

ACT III SCENE vi
OSD *Q adds 'and Abigall'*   36 fire.] ~,   37 close.] ~,   49 has] haa

ACT IV SCENE i
8 Master] Mʳ.   9 known?] ~ₔ   21 *Cazzo diabolo*] *Catho diabola*   22 Master] Mʳ.
65 *Jerusalem.*] ~,   68 Bullione] *Bullione*   103 him.] ~;   103SD *Exeunt*]
Exit (after ll.105)   107 Jacobines] *Jacobines*   111 *Jacomo*] *Jocome*   114 Turke]
Turke   119 *Jacomo*] *Jocoma*   133 is,] ~.   148 and] &
149 hang'd.] ~ₔ   155 Master] Mʳ.   161, 175 *Jacomo*] *Jocoma*   177 it,] ~ₔ
178, 193 Master] Mr.

ACT IV SCENE ii
OSD CURTEZANE] *Curtezant*   19 free-hold,] ~ₔ   fortie] 40   22 *Hodie*] *Hidie*
37 house; ~,   51, 76 and] &   81 Master] Mʳ.   85 three hundred] 300
89 all;] ~,   115, 116, 117, 118 and] &   120 and jeer'd] & ~   121 and
said] & ~   129, 130–1 five hundred] 500   131 one hundred] 100

ACT IV SCENE iii
1 three hundred] 300   2 Curtezane] *Curtezane*   5 him, . . . *Gorge* . . . that.]
~ₔ . . . ~, . . . ~ₔ   13 crosbiting;] ~ₔ   20 three hundred] 300   23–4 five
hundred] 500   29, 33 and] &   43 five hundred] 500   53 Sir,] ~ₔ
64 Three hundred] 300   five hundred] 500

ACT IV SCENE iv
6 CURTEZANE] *line attributed to 'Pil'*   25 alone?] ~.   32 incony] *incoomy*
49 chitterlins.] ~ ₔ   50 BARABAS] *Q omits speech-prefix, which is catchword on* H4ʳ
63 man?] ~.   72 circumcis'd.] ~ₔ   78 me] we

ACT V SCENE i
19SD BARABAS] *Jew*   20 dogs,] ~ₔ   23 sure.] ~,   35 Marry,] ~ₔ
38 what?] ~,   45SD *Exeunt*] *Exit*   93 five hundred] 500

ACT V SCENE ii
46 it.] ~ₔ   48 Governor—] ~ₔ   within;] ~,   104 towards *Ottoman.*]
toward, *Ottoman,*

ACT V SCENE iii
   OSD BASSOES] Bashawes   3 Towne,] ~.   8 *Mediterranean*] mediterranean
16 *Ottomen*] *Ottamon*   24 *Barabas,*] ~.   39 Bashawes] *Bashawes*   42 Lord.] ~,
43 Bashawes] *Bashawes*

ACT V SCENE v
   9 fill—and] ~ₐ~   50SD BASSOES] *Bashawes*   62SD *cut.*] ~,   63 this?] ~ₐ
66 treason, Bashawes flye] ~ₐ~, ~   72 Jew,] ~ₐ   77 breathe] breath
104 heardst] hardst   113 *Ottoman*] *Ottamen*   114 *Turkey*] Turkey   123 Fortune]
Fottune

APPENDIX—PROLOGUE TO THE STAGE
   5 *and*] and   12 merit] ~:

Lineation

Q's mislineations are so frequent as to demand a separate recording. They are obviously
the work of a careless or uncomprehending compositor.

ACT I SCENE i
   48–52 *Barabas,* | Thy . . . safe, riding . . . Rhode: | And . . . with . . . Merchandize |
Are . . . arriv'd, and . . . know | Whether . . . selfe will . . . them] *Barabas,* thy . . . safe, |
Riding . . . Rhode: And . . . Merchants |With . . . are . . . arriv'd | And . . . whether . . .
selfe | Will . . . them   69–70 And . . . not | Mine . . . *Alexandria*] And . . .
Alexandria

ACT I SCENE ii
   68–70 First, . . . be levyed . . . one halfe . . . estate] First, . . . be | Levyed . . . one |
Halfe . . . estate   73–4 Secondly, . . . become a Christian] Secondly, . . . become | A
Christian   199–201 I, I, | Pray . . . patience. You that | Were . . . want] I, I, pray . . .
patience. | You that were . . . want   274–5 Why so; | Then . . . house] Why so;
then . . . house   333–4 Why . . . *Abigall,* | What . . . thou amongst . . . Christians]
Why . . . *Abigall,* what . . . thou | Amongst . . . Christians

ACT II SCENE iii
   36–7 Now . . . Serpent then . . . foole] Now . . . Serpent | Then . . . foole   96–8
Come . . . price of . . . much] Come . . . price | Of . . . much   112–13 What . . .
hast, breake . . . thee] What . . . hast, | Breake . . . thee   117–18 A . . . Vanity if . . .
well] A . . . vanity | If . . . well   120–22 Some . . . colour of . . . goods. Tell
. . . well] Some . . . colour | Of . . . goods. | Tell . . . well   124–7 So . . . sickly, and
. . . day will . . . one that's . . . leaner] So . . . sickly, | And . . . day | Will . . . one |
That's . . . leaner   166–7 Faith . . . *Ithimer,* my . . . please] Faith . . . *Ithimer,* | My
. . . please   203–4 Faith, Master, | In . . . fire] Faith, Master, in . . . fire
359–60 You'll . . . friends? | Are . . . Jewes enow in *Malta*] You'll . . . friends? are . . .
Jewes | Enow in *Malta*   376–7 Feare . . . fire, | That he shall . . . him] Feare . . .
fire, that he | Shall . . . him

ACT III SCENE i
   17–23 Faith . . . Gardens I . . . counting-house where . . . I clamber'd . . . taking my . . .
tooke onely . . . man] Faith . . . Gardens | I . . . counting-house | Where . . . I |
Clamber'd . . . taking | My . . . tooke | Onely . . . man   25–6 Looke . . . away:
Zoons . . . keep'st, thou'lt . . . anon] Looke . . . away | Zoon's . . . keep'st | Thou'lt
. . . anon   27–30 O . . . is a . . . hundred of . . . Concubine] O . . . is | A . . . hun-
dred | Of . . . Concubine

ACT III SCENE iii

1–3 Why . . . villany, | So neatly plotted . . . perform'd? | Both . . . and flatly . . .
beguil'd] Why . . . villany, so neatly | Plotted . . . perform'd? both . . . and/Flatly . . .
beguil'd   9–11 Oh . . . subtil bottle-nos'd . . . had] Oh . . . subtil | Bottle-nos'd
. . . had   20–2 Why . . . it, and . . . *Mathias*] Why . . . it, | And . . . *Mathia*
36–7 A . . . sport with . . . then] A . . . sport | With . . . then

ACT III SCENE iv

39–41 Who . . . and throw . . . any thing . . . sake] Who . . . and | Throw . . . any |
Thing . . . sake   56–7 Well . . . brought the ladle . . . too] Well . . . brought | The
Ladle . . . too   58–60 Yes . . . devil had . . . Ladle] Yes . . . devil | Had . . . Ladle
65–8 Why . . . rice porredge . . . plump, and . . . aware] Why . . . rice | Porredge . . .
plump, | And . . . aware   108–9 What . . . of rice . . . it] What . . . of | Rice . . . it

ACT IV SCENE i

13–15 And . . . too; | But . . . hard by, | Good . . . Monks] And . . . too; but . . . hard |
By . . . Monks   19–21 No . . . long | An Hebrew borne . . . Christian. | *Cazzo dia-
bolo*] No . . . long an *Hebrew* | Borne . . . Christian. *Catho diabola*   155–7 Nay . . .
leane upon . . . Bacon] Nay . . . leane | Upon . . . Bacon   180–1 Good . . . but you
. . . escape] Good . . . but | You . . . escape   193–5 Fie . . . when holy . . . another]
Fie . . . when | Holy . . . another

ACT IV SCENE ii

6–8 I . . . of the . . . world] I . . . of | The . . . world   10–12 That . . . such a
. . . you] That . . . such | A . . . you   19–24 Upon . . . the gallowes . . . a Fryars
. . . hempen proverb . . . mercy of . . . where he comes] Upon . . . the | Gallowes . . . a |
Fryars . . . hempen | proverb . . . mercy | Of . . . where | He comes   25–43 I
. . . as this . . . was about . . . his hempen . . . if hee . . . whither he . . . haste: and . . . fellow met . . . and a . . . he gave . . . *Bellamira*, saluting . . . make cleane . . . that I . . . is; it
. . . in my . . . me ever . . . such love . . . now would . . . her] I . . . as | This . . . was |
About . . . his | Hempen . . . if | Hee . . . whither | He . . . haste: | And . . . fellow |
Met . . . and | A . . . he | Gave . . . *Bellamira*, | Saluting . . . make | Cleane . . . that | I .
. . is; | It . . . in | My . . . me | Ever . . . such | Love . . . now | Would . . . her
45–6 Gentleman . . . a poore . . . gone] Gentleman . . . a | Poore . . . gone.   48–9
Agen . . . sweet youth . . . letter] Agen . . . sweet | Youth . . . letter   50–2 I . . . my
selfe . . . service] I . . . my | Selfe . . . service   57–9 I'le . . . to make . . . hansome:
Pray . . . discharg'd] I'le . . . to | Make . . . hansome: | Pray . . . discharg'd   62–4
Nay . . . me; sweet . . . sake] Nay . . . me; | Sweet . . . sake   66–8 If . . . it; but . . .
doe their . . . earth] If . . . it; | But . . . doe | Their . . . earth   73–4 But . . . were
reveal'd . . . harme] But . . . were | Reveal'd . . . harme   75–6 I . . . more, I'le . . .
too] I . . . more, | I'le . . . too   85–7 I . . . this shall . . . so] I . . . this | Shall . . . so
89–90 Otherwise . . . a twinckle] Otherwise . . . a | Twinckle.   115–18 At . . .
turnd aside . . . thus; told . . . me] At . . . turnd | Aside . . . thus; | Told . . . me
123–4 The . . . thus: here's . . . not] The . . . thus: | Here's . . . not   126–8 But . . .
give me . . . for't] But . . . give | Me . . . for't   130–32 Sirra . . . crowns, and . . .
hav't] Sirra . . . crowns, | And . . . hav't   141–3 That . . . lips. What . . . me? It . . .
Starre] That . . . lips. | What . . . me? | It . . . Starre   146–7 That . . . together |
Afore we wake] That . . . together afore | We wake

ACT IV SCENE iii

26–7 Oh . . . see, there's . . . letter] Oh . . . see, | There's . . . letter
28–30 Might . . . him come . . . streight] Might . . . him | Come . . . streight   32–3
I . . . dine with . . . poyson'd] I . . . dine | With . . . poyson'd   37–8 Or . . . window:

you . . . meaning] Or . . . window: | You . . . meaning   39–41 I . . . your counting-house . . . thee] I . . . your | Counting-house . . . thee

ACT IV SCENE iv

23–4 I . . . he and . . . Fryar] I . . . he | And . . . Fryar   26–7 We . . . shall be . . . me] We . . . shall | Be . . . me   35–6 Wilt . . . a—pox . . . hick-up] Wilt . . . a— | Pox . . . hick-up   38–9 Prethe . . . me the . . . there] Prethe . . . me | The . . . there   58–9 You . . . of my Window] You . . . of | My Window   67–8 'Tis . . . upon pickled . . . Mushrumbs] 'Tis . . . upon | Pickled . . . Mushrumbs 69–70 What . . . this? The . . . doe] What . . . this? | The . . . doe   74–5 The . . . Elder when . . . himselfe] The . . . Elder | When . . . himselfe   77 A . . . is; whether . . . Fidler] A . . . is; | Whether . . . Fidler   82–6 No . . . now; bid . . . same token . . . *Bernardine* slept . . . clothes, any . . . it] No . . . now; | Bid . . . same | Token . . . *Bernardine* | Slept . . . clothes, | Any . . . it

ACT V SCENE i

12–15 Who . . . Gentlemen, poyson'd . . . Nuns, strangled . . . what mischiefe beside] Who . . . Gentlemen, | Poyson'd . . . Nuns, | Strangled . . . what | Mischiefe beside 17–18 Strong . . . my lodging . . . all] Strong . . . my | Lodging . . . all   30–2 Gilty . . . *Mathias* were . . . *Abigall*, he forg'd . . . challenge] Gilty . . . *Mathias* | Were . . . *Abigall*, | Forg'd . . . challenge   34–6 I . . . it? Marry . . . the Nuns . . . daughter] I . . it? | Marry . . . the | Nuns . . . daughter

ACT V SCENE v

58–9 I, *Barabas*, | Come . . . attend] I, *Barabas*, come . . . attend

COMMENTARY

Dramatis Personae

No such list is supplied in Q. The present one (original with this edition) mixes individual with functional names in accordance with the text's own usage.

1 MACHEVIL] Niccolo Machiavelli (1469–1527), a Florentine statesman and author of *Il Principe* and *Discorsi sopra la prima deca di Tito Livio*. *The Prince* was not published in English until 1640, but circulated in various manuscript versions before this date.

2 BARABAS] In the Bible, Barabbas—a murderer, according to St Mark (15: 7) and St Luke (23: 19); a robber (or rather a bandit: λῃστής, (*latro*) in St John's version (18: 40)—was released instead of Jesus. Hunter, 63–5, has shown how he came to be identified as *Antichristi typus* in patristic tradition.

3 ABIGALL] The name is translated in the Geneva Bible as 'the fathers joye'; in 1 Sam. 25 she is the peacemaking wife of Nabal, and some biblical commentators have seen her as the type of Jew who is converted to Christianity (cf. Hunter, 225 n. 55 = 80 n. 1).

4 ITHIMORE] One of the sons of Aaron was named Ithamar (Exod. 6: 23).

5 GOVERNOR] The role is that of the Grand Master of the Knights of Malta; the name 'Ferneze' seems to link Marlowe's character with the Farnese family—one of whose members was the Prince of Parma referred to at *Dr Faustus*, i. 93.

7 MATHIAS] Perhaps suggested by Matthias, brother of the Holy Roman Emperor Rudolf II and himself later to be emperor, who had served as governor-general of the Netherlands from 1578 to 1581; it was also the name of the apostle who took the place of Judas Iscariot (Acts 1: 26), and the great Hungarian king Matthias Corvinus (1458–90).

9 CALYMATH] Also called Selim-Calymath. Selim II (1566–74) was the son of Sultan Süleyman the Magnificent (1527–66), ruler of Turkey during the siege of Malta in 1565, but in fact took no part in it.

10 BASSO] The Ruskish *paşa*, in English 'pasha', a senior military officer; a variant spelling (used later in Q) is *Bashawe*.

15 PILIA-BORZA] Pick purse (Italian *pigliaborza*, 'purse-taker').

Prologue

1 An epigram by Gabriel Harvey, '*Machiavellus ipse loquitur*' (1578) is translated by Michel Poirier, *Christopher Marlowe* (London, Chatto & Windus, 1951), 48–9.

3 the *Guize* is dead] On 23 December NS 1588 Henri de Lorraine, third duke of Guise, the leader of the militant Roman Catholic *Ligue*, who was subsidized by Spain and had designs on the throne of France, was summoned to the royal chamber at Blois and there assassinated on the orders of King Henri III, much to the relief of Protestant England. Marlowe dramatized the event in *The Massacre at Paris*. By alluding to it, Machevil makes his point that princes in the real world need to display the craft and ruthlessness he advocates.

10 some . . . bookes] Donne attributes the same behaviour to the Roman Catholics:

He, whom they that even hate his name, (our Adversaries of the Roman perswasion) doe yet so far tacitly reverence, as that, though they will not name him, they will transfer, and insert his expositions of Scriptures, into their works, and passe them as their owne, that is *Calvin*.

The Sermons of John Donne, ed. G. R. Potter and E. M. Simpson 10 vols. (Berkeley and Los Angeles, University of California Press, 1953–62), vol. viii, Sermon No. 14, p. 314.

12 *Peters* Chayre] The papacy. 'As for the Popes, most of them haue clymbed up to the Holy See by lyes, hypocrisie, guiles and deceipt, by money, armes, massacres, poysonings and Magicall arts' (*The Restorer of the French Estate* (London, 1589), cit. Paul H. Kocher, *Christopher Marlowe: A Study of his Thought, Learning, and Character* (Chapel Hill: University of North Carolina Press, 1946), 197).

16 Birds of the Aire] The murder of Ibycus was brought to light through the agency of a flock of cranes (Plutarch, *De garrulitate* 14).

19 *Caesar*] In *Discourses* i. 29, Machiavelli describes Caesar as a tyrant who seized power by force.

Empery] Reed's emendation of Q 'Empire' completes the scansion of the line, using the form usually preferred by Marlowe (cf. *1 Tamburlaine*, v. i. 352).

21 *Draco*] Draco was an Athenian legislator; the laws he codified for the citizens of Athens *c.*621 BC were said, on account of their severity, to be written in letters of blood.

22 Citadell] In *The Prince*, ch. xx, Machiavelli recommends the use of citadels for protection against rebellious citizens.

23 import] *OED* 9, 'To obtain, gain, win (victory)'.

24 maxime] Trisyllabic, cf. *Dr Faustus* v. 223: 'whose termine is tearm'd the worlds wide pole'.

24 *Phaleris*] Phalaris, a Sicilian tyrant 570–554 BC who roasted his enemies in an oven shaped like a bull—and perished himself in the same way, overthrown by revolutionaries.

26 wites] Marlowe paraphrases the 'base concepted witts' with which he rendered Ovid's *vilia miretur vulgus* (*Elegies* I. xv, 35), although Ovid's contempt is for the common herd and Marlowe's apparently for the minds that have low thoughts and cannot rise above the commonplace. The ambiguous 'wites' was interpreted as 'wights' by Reed (followed by Bawcutt), but as 'wits' by Shone (followed by Craik), which seems more appropriate to the context.

29 *Britanie*] Bullen's emendation of Q 'Britaine' is justified on metrical grounds and as being Marlowe's own preferred spelling (cf. *Edward II*, II. ii. 42: 'the proudest peere of *Britanie*').

30 present] Machevil presents 'the Tragedy of a Jew' just as the Chorus presents the tragedy of Dr Faustus (and as the medieval 'Doctors' presented the Morality plays).

33 Grace] *OED* 2, 'To show favour or be gracious to'.

35 favours] Both *OED* 4, 'to side with, take the part of'; and *OED* 8, 'to resemble'.

Act I scene i

OSD *Enter* BARABAS] Such a 'discovery' entrance at the beginning of the play is favoured by Marlowe in *Dido Queene of Carthage* and *Dr Faustus*.

4 Samnites] A tribe of central Italy, conquered by the Romans and referred to by Lucan in *Bellum Civile* ii. 137.

men of *Uzz*] 'There was a man in the land of Uz called Iob', Job I: I.

6 silverlings] The word (from Luther's *Silberling*) is used by Tyndale and Coverdale to denote the chief silver coin in Hebrew currency (the shekel) or in Roman (the denarius, conventionally rendered 'penny'—hence Barabas's 'paltry').

19 Indian Mynes] Cf. *1 Tamburlaine*, II. v. 41: 'Then will we march to all those Indian Mines'. *OED* cites *Purchas his Pilgrimage* (1614) to illustrate the confusion of senses of *India*: 'The name of India, is now applied to all farre-distant Countries, not in the extreme limits of Asia alone; but even to whole America, through the errour of

Columbus . . . who . . . in the Westerne world, thought that they had met with Ophir, and the Indian regions of the East.'

25–7 Bags . . . Diamonds] In the Croxton *Play of the Sacrament*, the Jew Jonathas boasts that he has

> dyamantys derewourthy to dresse,
> And emerawdys, ryche I trow they be,
> Onyx and achatys both more and lesse,
> Topazyouns, smaragdys of grete degre,
> Perlys precyous grete plente,
> Of rubes ryche I have grete renown;
> Crepawdys and calcedonyes semely to se,
> And curyous carbunclys here ye fynd mown . . .

By contrast, however, the Old Testament Job, cataloguing all precious stones and metals, declares that the price of wisdom is above all these (Job 28: 15 ff).

28 seildsene] seldom seen, rare.

29 indifferently rated] fairly valued. Cf. I. ii. 185, V. iii. 29.

30 Carrect] An obsolete form of 'carat' = a very small measure of weight used for diamonds and other precious stones.

33 ware wherein] Marlowe may well not have distinguished *w* and *wh*. Cf. Sir John Davies, *Orchestra* (1596), 232–3:

> Behold the world how it is whirled round
> And for it is so whirl'd, is named so.

His and his contemporaries' love of soundplay suggests that the collocation may be deliberate, but Marlowe may have been more concerned with the alliteration 'ware . . . wealth'.

37 Infinite . . . roome] The notion is commonplace (Tilley, W921: 'Great worth is often found in things of small appearance'). Hunter (pp. 221–5 = 75–80) suggests that the line 'draws on two persistent images of Christ *in utero Virginis*'.

39 Halcions bill] Sir Thomas Browne notes as a common error 'that a Kingfisher hanged by the bill, sheweth in what quarter the wind is, by an occult and secret propriety, converting the breast to that point of the Horizon from whence the wind doth blow' (*Pseudodoxia Epidemica*, III. x, ed. Robin Robbins, 2 vols. (Oxford University Press, 1981), i. 196).

46 *Candie*] Crete (Italian *Candia*).

49 Rhode] *OED* 3 explains this as the 'roadstead, a sheltered stretch of water beyond the harbour but close to the land'.

52 custome] *OED* 3 offers Marlowe's line as one of the rare examples of the verb meaning 'to pay duty or toll on'.

78 crazed] unsound; Marlowe uses this adjective with reference to buildings in *The Massacre at Paris* (xii. 1201), and *Edward II* (I. iv. 100).

86 Orient] *OED* distinguishes between the pearls found in the Indian seas and those, less beautiful, from European oysters (*orient* 2b).

100 trowles] *OED* 8, 'To come in abundantly like a flowing stream'.

102 Blessings promis'd to the Jewes] The Book of Genesis tells of the covenant made between God and the Hebrew patriarch Abram: 'And I wil make my couenant betwene me and thee, and I wil multiply thee exceadingly' (17: 2).

103 *Abrams*] Abraham's. When the covenant was first made, the name of the patriarch was changed: 'Nether shal thy name anie more be called Abrám, but thy name shalbe Abrahám: for a father of manie nacions haue I made thee' (Gen. 17: 5).

104 men] The syntax seems to demand Shone's emendation from Q's 'man'.

106 Ripping the bowels of the earth] Barabas seems to approve the exploitation of natural resources which more conservationist poets deplored; cf. *The Faerie Queene*, II. VII. xvii.

> Then gan a cursed hand the quiet wombe
> Of his great Grandmother with steele to wound,
> And the hid treasures in her sacred tombe
> With Sacriledge to dig.

107 Seas . . . servants] An emendation is surely necessary for Q's 'Sea . . . servants', and Broughton's plural 'seas . . . servants' seems more appropriate to the speech than Shone's singular 'sea . . . servant'.

113 fruits . . . faith] 'Therefore by their frutes ye shal knowe them' (Matt. 7: 20).

115 profession] *OED* 5 'The profession of religion; the declaration of belief in and obedience to religion.'

116 Happily . . . haplesse] cf. l. 33.

117 for his conscience lives in beggery] The Second Murderer in *Richard III* observes that conscience 'beggars any man that keeps it' (I. iv. 140).

118 scatter'd Nation] The Jewish diaspora was foretold by Moses in the Book of Deuteronomy: 'thou . . . shalt be scatered through all the kingdomes of the earth.' (28: 25).

119 scambled] *OED* 6, 'To collect in a haphazard or irregular manner'.

121–2 *Kirriah Jairim . . . Obed* in *Bairseth*] Marlowe seems to be creating an individual from the name of a city, Kiriáth-iearím (1 Chron. 2: 50). The same source could have suggested the name of Obed to Marlowe (he was the father of Jesse, 1 Chron. 2: 12). The unidentified place-name could be a corruption of Baaseiáh (1 Chron. 6: 40).

122 *Nones*] The Nunes family were Portuguese Marranos—Jews who had been compelled to accept the Christian faith. One of these was Hector Nunez (1521–91), who had some connection with Elizabeth I's government, passing military and diplomatic information through his continental agents (see Lucien Wolf, 'Jews in Elizabethan England', *Transactions of the Jewish Historical Society of England*, 11 (1924–7), 8–9).

135 *Agamemnon*] The Greek leader sacrificed his daughter Iphigenia to the goddess Artemis in order to obtain a fair wind to sail to Troy. The story is told by Ovid in *Metamorphoses*, xii. 29 ff.:

As soone as pitie yeelded had to cace of publicke weele,
And reason got the upper hand of fathers loving zeale,
So that the Ladye Iphigen before the altar stood
Among the weeping ministers, to give her maydens blood . . .

Ovid's *Metamorphoses*, trans. Arthur Golding (1567), ed. John Frederick Nims (New York, 1965), 300, ll. 31–4.
The irony implicit in the comparison is typical of Marlowe: Agamemnon's love for his daughter was unquestionable, but his love for his country was greater and demanded the sacrifice of Iphigenia. And Barabas's daughter Abigall will also be sacrificed.

137 *policie*] One of the most charged words in the English language, whose sense ranges from the neutrality of *OED* 1, 'An organized and established system of government'; to *OED* 4b, 'A device, expedient, contrivance; a crafty device, stratagem, trick.'

173 *Zaareth . . . Temanite*] Job's three friends—Eliphaz the Temanite, Zophar, and Bildad—provided the inspiration for this episode, and may well have done something to suggest names for Marlowe's Jews (Job 2: 11).

182 *the Towne*] Early maps of Malta mark 'Oppidum' or 'Città' in the centre of the island, indicating the position of Mdina: see Introduction, p. xi.

186 *Ego . . . proximus*] The phrase, originating with Terence (*Andria* 636: *Proximus sum egomet mihi*), became a by-word for selfishness in English: 'I am always nearest to myself' (Tilley, N57).

Act I scene ii

OSD GOVERNOR] The plural 'Governors' is sometimes to be found in this scene (see 'Accidental Emendations'). This would seem to be a printer's error rather than (as Bennett suggested) a misconception of Marlowe's which he abandoned in later scenes.

3 *Cyprus*] Like Rhodes, Cyprus was conquered by the Turks in the sixteenth century.

23 *Callapine*] Marlowe uses the name of Bajazeth's son from Part 2 of *Tamburlaine*; it was perhaps suggested by 'Calepine', the standard Latin dictionary of the time.

45 longs] belongs.

47 cast] calculated.

48 the warres]. History gives no authority for the Governor's excuse; after their expulsion from Rhodes in 1522, the Knights of the Order of St John seem to have supported their continued existence in Malta by organized piracy.

64 accursed in the sight of heaven] The Jews took upon themselves the responsibility for Christ's crucifixion: 'Then answered all the people, and said, His blood be on vs, and on our children' (Matt. 27: 25).

79 earth-mettall'd] having the dull, spiritless temperament (mettle) which arises from the dry cold of elemental earth.

85 doe] In emending Q's 'did', suggesting a compositorial misreading, Craik draws attention to Luke 23: 34, 'Father, forgiue them, for they knowe not what thei do'.

91 *Corpo di dio*] By God's body.

99–100 better one . . . private man] The same doctrine was articulated by the high priest, Caiaphas, to justify the killing of Jesus: 'it is expedient for vs, that one man dye for the people, and that the whole nacion perish not' (John 11: 50). Tilley O42 offers a proverbial form: 'Better one die than all'.

105 nought . . . nothing] The earliest formulation of this principle seems to be that of Xenophanes in the sixth century BC: *Die Fragmente der Vorsokratiker*, ed. H. Diels, rev. W. Kranz (6th and later edns.), 21 A 28. 2. But closer in form are Lucretius i. 150 and Persius iii. 84. See too Tilley, N285.

108 your first curse] See l. 64 *n.*

109 poore and scorn'd] The line seems to quote the words of Isaiah describing one 'despised and reiected of men' (53: 3).

111 Scripture] Tilley, D230, 'The Devil can cite scripture for his purpose'. Shakespeare's lines in *The Merchant of Venice* read like a comment on Marlowe's line:

> The devil can cite Scripture for his purpose.
> An evil soul producing holy witness
> Is like a villain with a smiling cheek,
> A goodly apple rotten at the heart.
> O, what a goodly outside falsehood hath!
>   (I. iii. 98–102.)

115 cast away] damned.

116 transgression] Isa. 53: 8: 'for the transgression of my people was he plagued'.

117 dealeth righteously] 'The treasures of wickednes profite nothing: but righteousnes deliuereth from death' (Prov. 10: 2).

123–6 covetousnesse . . . theft] The antagonists swop Commandments: the tenth, 'Thou shalt not couet thy neighbours house . . . nether any thing that is thy neighbours', and the eighth, 'Thou shalt not steale' (Exod. 20: 17, 15).

127 compasse] *OED* 2, 'To contrive, devise, machinate (a purpose). Usually in a bad sense.'

135 the other] i.e. the other Jews.

136 Then . . . residue] The Officer would have no authority of his own, so I have followed Robinson in allocating this line to the Governor. The remainder of the tribute-money will be raised by the Knights from outside Malta.

144 staine our hands] The Governor assumes Pilate's role (Matt. 27: 24): 'When Pilate sawe that he auailed nothing, but that more tumulte was made, he toke water and wasshed his hands before the multitude, saying, I am innocent of the blood of this iust man: loke you to it.'

153 right . . . wrong] *summum ius, summa iniuria* (Cicero, *De officiis*, i. 33).

161 simplicity . . . suggest] The Knights of St John should, by their Order, have espoused 'the simplicitie that is in Christ' (2 Cor. 11: 3).

162 plagues of *Egypt*] These are described in Exod. 7–12; the whole land of Egypt was afflicted because Pharaoh would not release the Israelites from bondage.

164 *Primus Motor*] The concept of God as the First Mover, moving all things else, is Aristotelian (*Metaphysics*, xii. 6); cf. 1 *Tamburlaine*, IV. ii. 8–9:

The chiefest God, first moover of that Spheare
Enchac'd with thousands ever shining lamps . . .

166 banne] curse.

174 brooke] endure.

181 *Job*] Job 1: 3: 'His substance also was seuen thousand shepe,
and thre thousand camels, and fyue hundreth yoke of oxen, and fyue
hundreth she asses . . . so that this man was the greatest of all the
men of the East.' Bawcutt suggests that Q's 'two' in l. 183 may be a
misreading of 'v'.

191–5 Job 3: 1–10: 'Afterward Iob opened his mouthe, and cursed
his day. And Iob cryed out, and said, Let the daye perish, wherein I
was borne, and the night when it was said, There is a manchilde con-
ceiued. Let that day be darkenes, let not God regarde if from aboue,
nether let the light shine vpon it, But let darkenes, & the shadowe of
death staine it: let the cloude remaine vpon it, & let them make it
fearefull as a bitter day . . . Yea, desolate be that night . . . Because it
shut not vp the dores of my mothers wombe: nor hid sorowe from
mine eyes.'

196–8 Job 7: 3: 'So haue I had as an inheritance the moneths of
vanitie, and peineful nights haue bene appointed vnto me'.

207 Job 7: 11: 'Therefore I wil not spare my mouthe, but wil
speake in the trouble of my spirit, & muse in the bitternes of my
minde.'

221 reaching] foreseeing.

222 cast] forecast.

234 rent] A variant form of 'rend'.

235 reduce] *OED* 9c, 'redress, repair'; Marlowe's usage is the only
example cited by *OED*.

236–7 past . . . exclamations] Tilley, C921, 'Past cure, past care'.

238 sufferance breeds ease] Tilley, S955, 'Sufferance breeds ease'.

244 Portagues] Portuguese gold coins.

254 sect] sex.

255 generally] without exception.

279–80 Religion . . . suspition] Cf. *Richard III*, III. vii, where
Richard enters '*between two* Bishops'.

282 precise] *OED* 2, 'strict in the observance of rule'.

299 not necessary I be seene] i.e. necessary that I should not be seen.

302 new made Nunnery] The repetition of this phrase at l. 307, the
confusion of prefixes at ll. 303 and 309, and the careless stage direc-

tion at l. 301 (Q *three* ... *two*) suggest to Bawcutt (who read *two* ... *three*) that the passage was 'hastily written and not revised'.

307 waters] On a Mediterranean island like Malta, the water-supplies are of prime importance.

310 you] Craik reads 'yon', suggesting that Abigall is addressing the Abbasse as the spiritual 'guide' of the other Nun[s].

313 hopelesse ... haplesse] Cf. *The Spanish Tragedy*, IV. iv. 84: 'The hopeless father of a hapless son'.

323 of the spirit] by divine influence; cf. John 3: 5–6: 'except that a man be borne of water and of the Spirit, he can not enter into the kingdome of God. That which is borne of the flesh, is flesh: & that that is borne of the Spirit, is spirit.'

324 a moving spirit] The First Fryar responds seriously, but his solemnity is undercut by his colleague's bawdy innuendo.

335 man of little faith] A regular Christian apostrophe (e.g. Matt. 6: 30).

336 mortified her selfe] made herself dead to worldly desires and temptations, as recommended in the Epistle to the Romans: 'if ye mortifie the dedes of the bodie by the Spirit, ye shal liue' (8: 30).

338 Child of perdition] In St John's Gospel (17: 12) the phrase seems to be applied to the treacherous Judas Iscariot.

342 give me] Abigall asks for her father's blessing.

344SD I follow Bawcutt in assuming that here, as at l. 350, a gesture is called for; and so I mark Q's obelus. Barabas's blasphemy is comic and obvious.

Act I scene iii

As the stage empties with the departure of Barabas and Abigall, it seems appropriate to begin a new scene here.

10 in a dump] depressed.

15 *Citherea's*] Cytherea is the goddess Venus, so called from the island of Cythera. Mathias's eulogy seems to glance back (through the notion of metamorphosis) to Ovid's tale of the rape of Proserpina, *Metamorphoses*, V. 391 ff.

> While in this garden Proserpine was taking hir pastime,
> In gathering eyther Violets blew, or Lillies white as Lime,
> And while of Maidenly desire she fillde hir Maund and Lap,
> Endevoring to outgather hir companions there, by hap
> Dis spide hir: lovde hir: caught hir up ...
>
>   (Golding, 126, ll. 491–5)

22 countermur'd] doubly walled for defence. Q's 'countermin'd'
here, and 'contermin'd' at v. iii. 9. could be simple misreadings of MS;
the correction was made in both places by Collier, and independently
by K. Deighton, *The Old Dramatists: Conjectural Readings* (West-
minster: Archibald Constable and Co., 1896), 120–1.

walls of brasse] Cf. *Dr Faustus*, i. 88: 'Ile have them wall all
Jermany with brasse'; Greene's Friar Bacon planned 'to circle
England round with brass' (*Friar Bacon and Friar Bungay*, ii. 29), and
Spenser's Merlin 'did intend, A brasen wall in compas to compile
About *Cairmardin*' (*The Faerie Queene*, III. III. x. 2–4).

Act II scene i

1 sad presaging Raven] Because the raven flew behind marching
armies in anticipation of corpses, it became recognized as a bird of ill-
omen: cf. *Macbeth*:

> The raven himself is hoarse
> That croaks the fatal entrance of Duncan
> Under my battlements.   (I. v. 38–40)

2 passeport] *OED* 2b, 'A permit for discharged inmates of a hospi-
tal, soldiers . . . to proceed to a specified destination'.

11 further comfort] additional compensation; cf. Gaveston's rejec-
tion of the soldier in *Edward II*: 'Why there are hospitals for such as
you' (I. i. 36).

12–13 piller] When the Israelites escaped from Egypt, 'the Lord
went before them . . . by night in a piller of fyre' (Exod. 13: 21).

14 *Abrahams* off-spring] The Jews trace their descent back to the
patriarch Abraham, claiming their inheritance through Isaac and his
son Jacob (who was surnamed Israel). The history is told in the Book
of Genesis.

25 wealth] Bullen emends to 'youth'; but story-telling was not only
for children.

25 winters tales] Cf. *Richard II*:

> In winter's tedious nights sit by the fire
> With good old folks, and let them tell thee tales
> Of woeful ages long ago betid.   (v. i. 40–2)

26 spirits and ghosts] Cf. *Hamlet*:

> . . . if thou hast uphoarded in thy life
> Extorted treasure in the womb of earth,
> For which they say you spirits oft walk in death,
> Speak of it, stay and speak.   (I. i. 136–9)

Cf. also Ben Jonson, *Every Man Out of His Humour*: 'Well now! Shall my sonne gain a benevolence by my death? or any body be the better for my gold, or so forth? No. Aliue, I kept it from 'hem, and (dead) my ghost shall walke about it, and preserue it . . .' (III. vii. 63–5).

35–6 gentle sleepe . . . *Morpheus*] Morpheus, 'the feyner of mannes shape, a craftye lad' was one of the sons of Somnus, god of sleepe; in *Metamorphoses* xi. 633 ff. he is sent to Alcyone at the request of Juno (ll. 735 ff. in Golding).

37 walke] Broughton suggested an emendation to 'wake', which has been accepted by some editors.

39 The Spanish phrase sounds proverbial—but is still obscure. Craik modernizes to *Bueno para todos mi ganado no era*, and translates 'My flock was not good for all'; Bawcutt has ' "Bien para todos mi ganada no es" ' and glosses ' "My gain is not good for everybody" (with the implication "I don't want to hand over the money I have gained for everybody")'.

41 starre . . . East] The magi seeking the King of the Jews told Herod 'we have sene his starre in the East' (Matt. 2: 2).

42 Loadstarre] guiding star.

46–7 girle . . . gold] The words are nearly echoed by Shylock in *The Merchant of Venice* when he laments his loss: 'My daughter! O my ducats! O my daughter!' (II. viii. 15).

49 first beginner . . . blisse] Barabas is obliquely blasphemous. God is the First Beginner, and *OED* defines *bliss* 2c as 'The perfect joy of Heaven'. Cf. Volpone's matins hymn to his gold: 'Open the shrine, that I may see my saint' (Ben Jonson, *Volpone*, I. i. 2).

52 practise] *OED* 8b, 'plan, devise means for'; and also, perhaps, sense 9, 'use stratagem or artifice'.

54 midnight] In the early Christian church, and afterwards by some churches, the office of Matins was performed at midnight; however, it is more relevant that by poetic and dramatic convention dawn may follow hard on midnight: see Virgil, *Aeneid*, v. 738–9

> torquet medios Nox umida cursus
> et me saevus equis Oriens adflavit anhelis.

So in *Hamlet*, I. iii. 196–220 the ghost of Hamlet's father appears 'in the dead waste and middle of the night', walks slowly three times past the guards, and disappears when 'the morning cock crew loud'.

59 *Phoebus*] Phoebus Apollo, the sun-god of classical mythology; Barabas speaks in traditional *aubade* language; cf. *Cymbeline*:

> Hark, hark, the lark at heaven's gate sings,
> And Phoebus gins arise,
> His steeds to water at those springs
> On chalic'd flow'rs that lies;
> And winking Mary-buds begin
> To ope their golden eyes.
>
> (II. iii. 19–24)

63 *Hermoso . . . Dineros*] The Spanish phrase is well rendered by a line from Arthur Hugh Clough: 'How pleasant it is to have money, heigh ho!' (*Dipsychus*).

Act II scene ii

7 Catholike King] A traditional title of the kings of Spain, conferred upon them by Pope Alexander VI in 1494.

11 vail'd] *OED* vail, 'to lower one's sails in token of respect or submission'.

Turkish] Q's '*Spanish*' is perhaps an authorial mistake, rather than a misreading of secretary hand.

14 luft, and tackt] Del Bosco describes the zigzag movement of his sailing-ship, sailing with and against the wind to outmanœuvre the oar-driven galleys.

23 Tributary league] There is no grounding in fact for the treaty of friendship (with payment of tribute) between the Knights and the Turks.

31 *Rhodes*] The Knights of St John were based in Rhodes from 1309 until their expulsion by Süleyman II in 1522; this was an honourable defeat for the Knights, but perhaps an embarrassment for the European countries that failed to supply aid.

32 stated here] In 1530 the Knights were established in Malta by the Emperor Charles V, who was also King Charles I of Spain.

38 them] The emendation of Q's 'you' is justifiable on grounds of sense; the king of Spain would not have wanted to expel the Knights from Malta.

50 not a man surviv'd] Historically this is not accurate. With their Grand Master, Villiers de L'Isle Adam, the Knights were driven from Rhodes and forced to seek for another sanctuary.

54 bullets wrapt in smoake and fire] Shakespeare perhaps recalled the image in *King John*, where he refers to 'bullets wrapp'd in fire' (II. i. 227).

Act II scene iii

6 SD] The anticipatory direction *Ent. Bar.* at l. 4 perhaps suggests the work of a book-keeper.

7–8 swine-eating ... circumciz'd] In thus anathematizing the Christians, Barabas identifies himself racially. Meat from the pig was forbidden ('and the swine ... he shalbe vncleane to you', Lev. 11: 7) to the Jews, who were told by Moses that they were a nation specially chosen by the Almighty: 'For thou art an holy people vnto the Lord thy God, the Lord thy God hathe chosen thee, to be a precious people vnto him selfe, aboue all people that are vpon the earth' (Deut. 7: 6). The Lord also ordained the circumcision of the Jews: 'it shal be a signe of the couenant betwene me and you' (Gen. 17: 11).

10 *Titus* and *Vespasian*] The emperor Vespasian and his son Titus managed the siege and destruction of Jerusalem in AD 70.

18 the tribe of *Levy*] the tribe of Levi was properly the priestly caste, but loosely used by Gentiles for Jews in general. The Levite of Judges 19 (cf. l. 303 n.) did not forgive an injury; but as Van Fossen observes, the Levites held jurisdiction over the cities of refuge that sheltered accidental homicides (Joshua 20–1). Bawcutt suggests that Marlowe may also have had in mind John of Salisbury, *Policraticus*, iv. 6, ed. C. C. I. Webb (Oxford: Clarendon Press, 1909), i. 521, which cites Deut. 17: 18 and holds up for imitation the priests of the tribe of Levi:

> But who are priests of the tribe of Levi? Those, namely, who without the incentive of avarice, without the motive of ambition, without affectation of flesh and blood have been introduced into the Church by law. And not the law of the letter, which mortifieth, but the law of the spirit, which in holiness of mind, cleanness of body, purity of faith and works of charity, giveth life.
>
> *The Statesman's Book of John of Salisbury*, trans. J. Dickinson (New York: A. A. Knopf, 1927), 25.

20 fawne like Spaniels] Cf. *A Midsummer Night's Dream*:

> I am your spaniel; and, Demetrius,
> The more you beat me, I will fawn on you.
>
> (II. i. 203–4.)

21 when we grin we bite] Cf. *Richard III*:

> O Buckingham, take heed of yonder dog!
> Look when he fawns he bites; and when he bites,
> His venom tooth will rankle to the death.
>
> (I. iii. 288–90).

23 *Florence*] The home of Machiavelli.

26 stall] Barnabe Barnes, *The Devils Charter* (London: J. Wright, 1607), refers to drunkards who 'driueling sleepe on euery stall and bench' (F2ᵛ).

36–7 more of the Serpent then the Dove] Cf. Matt. 10: 16: 'be ye therefore wise as serpentes, and innocent as doues.'

37 more knave than foole] Tilley, K129.

48 the Promise] Barabas speaks of the bond between God and the Jews: 'Moreouer I wil establish my couenant betwene me and thee, and thy sede after thee in their generacions, for an euerlasting couenant' (Gen. 17: 7). Cf. also Ps. 105: 8, 'He hathe alwaie remembred his couenant & promes, that he made to a thousand generacions'.

53 sacrifice her on a pile of wood] Barabas offers to imitate Abraham, who was prepared thus to sacrifice his son Isaac (Gen. 22); and Agamemnon, who sacrificed his daughter Iphigenia in the same way (cf. I. i. 140).

54 poyson of the City] Craik suggests that this was the plague.

55 White leprosie] The skin-disease (characterised by a white scaliness) was the horror of the Israelites (Levi. 13).

56 foile] The word's multiplicity of meanings includes *OED* 5, 'A thin leaf of some metal placed under a precious stone to increase its brilliancy'. Lodowicke implies that Abigall needs a husband to set her off to best advantage—as Leander argued in Marlowe's poem:

> mayds are nothing then,
> Without the sweet societie of men.
> *Hero and Leander*, 255–6.

Barabas takes up later senses (*OED* 6, 7) of 'defile' and 'dishonour'.

60 square or pointed] On the cutting of diamonds, *OED* cites Mandeville: 'Thei ben square and poynted of here owne kynde.'

63 *Cinthia's*] the moon's.

71 ruth] compassion.

73 Catechising] teaching by oral instruction.

102–7 Bennett glosses the passage thus: 'If he has a new way of purse-stealing, he is worth three hundred plates, provided that a perpetual pardon or charter with the town-seal upon it can be got to keep him from the gallows, since the Sessions-days are crucial to thieves, and few or none escape except they are purged of their offences'.

103, 108 plats] pieces of silver or gold.

106 criticall] *OED* 4, 'Relating to the crisis or turning-point of a disease; determining the issue of a disease, etc'.

112 Philosophers stone] The 'famous stone That turneth all to gold' (George Herbert) was much sought after by alchemists in the sixteenth and seventeenth centuries.

117–18 Lady Vanity] One of the traditional misleaders of Youth (Juventus); a dramatic presentation is offered in the morality play of 'The Marriage of Wit and Wisdom', which is performed in Act IV of *The Booke of Sir Thomas Moore* (ed. V. Gabriele and G. Melchiori, Manchester University Press, 1989).

125–7 Cf. Shylock's complaint that Launcelot Gobbo is 'a huge feeder' (*The Merchant of Venice*, II. v. 46).

130 *Trace*] The Thracians were notoriously savage warriors.

155 Comment on the *Machabees*] The two apocryphal books of Maccabees narrate the Jewish national liberation in the second century BC.

177 poyson wells] Rumours of Jewish well-poisoning were rife in Europe in the thirteenth and fourteenth centuries (associating Jews with the spread of the Black Death); cf. Joshua Trachtenberg, *The Devil and the Jews* (New Haven: Yale University Press, 1943).

185 in ure] in practice.

188 warres 'twixt *France* and *Germanie*] The struggle between Francis I of France and the Habsburg Emperor Charles V, and their successors Henry II and Ferdinand I, continued intermittently from 1519 until a peace-treaty was signed in 1559.

193 Brokery] *OED*'s sense 1, 'the business or action of a broker', was not yet distinguished from sense 3, 'rascally dealing or trafficking'.

224 *Ormus*] Hormuz, a town on the Persian Gulf, famous as a jewel-market.

229 Philistine] In the Old Testament, the Philistines were the traditional enemies of the Jews; cf. 1 Samuel 17.

231 seed of *Abraham*] For the Jewish boast of descent from the patriarch, cf. Ps. 105: 6: 'Ye sede of Abrahám his seruant, ye children of Iaakób, which are his elect.'

237 made sure] betrothed.

249 heaven rain'd Manna for the Jewes] In the wilderness, the children of Israel were fed with a divinely supplied substance: 'And when

the dewe that was fallen was ascended, beholde, a smale rounde thing was vpon the face of the wildernes, smale as the hore frost on the earth' (Exod. 16: 14).

294 Win it, and weare it] proverbial (Tilley, W408)

unsoyl'd] Collier's conjectural emendation to 'unfoiled' (involving a long-*s*/*f* substitution) would allow a continuation of the word-play in l. 56; but such extended jokes are not characteristic of Marlowe's style.

297–8 golden crosse . . . ring] Gold coins current in Marlowe's day were stamped with a circled cross, and engraved around the circumference with Christian mottoes. Bawcutt thinks that the 'posies' might refer to the verses engraved on wedding-rings at this time (as in Middleton's *A Chaste Maid in Cheapside*, I. i. 188–91).

302 off-spring of *Caine*] In *Antiquities of the Jews* (I. ii. 2, § 66), Flavius Josephus recounts how 'even while *Adam* was alive, it came to pass, that the posterity of *Cain* became exceedingly wicked, every one successively dying one after another more wicked than the former: they were intolerable in war, and vehement in robberies; and if any one were slow to murder people, yet was he bold in his profligate behaviour; in acting unjustly, and in doing injuries for gain' (*Works of Josephus*, trans. W. Whiston (London: J. Whiston, 1737, i. 7).

Jebusite] A gloss in the Geneva Bible on Judg. 19: 11–12 identifies these (the original inhabitants of Jerusalem, 'not of the children of Israel') as 'them that professed not the true God'.

303 tasted of the Passeover] The Passover meal, ordained by the Almighty (Exodus 12), is the chief Jewish festival and celebrates the Jews' deliverance from bondage in Egypt.

304 land of *Canaan*] This was promised to the Jews as part of God's covenant recorded in Gen. 17: 8.

305 *Messias*] The older (Graeco-Latin) form of 'Messiah'.

306 gentle Magot] A 'gentle' (*OED* 2) is the larva of the bluebottle (= maggot). Barabas's 'gentle'/'gentile' pun is also to be found in *The Merchant of Venice* in Gratiano's praise of Jessica as 'a gentle and no Jew' (II. vi. 51).

312 Faith . . . Heretickes] Cf. *2 Tamburlaine*, where Marlowe transfers to the battle of Nicopolis (1396) the breach of faith with the Turk induced (with disastrous outcome) by the papal legate in the Varna campaign of 1444:

> with such Infidels,
> In whom no faith nor true religion rests,

We are not bound to those accomplishments,
The holy lawes of Christendome injoine:

(II. i. 33–41.)

Tilley gives the phrase as proverbial (F33), but quotes no example earlier than Marlowe's usage. However, Thomas Lupton declared, in *A Persuasion from Papistrie* (London: H. Bynneman, 1581), 44 that 'it is a maxime and a rule with the Pope and his partakers that *Fides non est seruanda haereticis*'. See F. P. Wilson, *Shakespearian and Other Studies*, ed. Helen Gardner (Oxford: Clarendon Press, 1969), 162.

343 accessary.] *OED* quotes Blackstone's legal definition: 'He who is not the chief actor in the offence, nor present at its performance, but in some way concerned therein, either before or after the fact committed.'

Act III scene i

1 Since . . . besieg'd] In the play, the siege of the island does not properly start until the end of Act III scene v, and Bennett suggested that there might have been some textual rearrangement; but it seems enough to assume, with Bawcutt, 'that the presence of the Turkish fleet near Malta has had the effect of a blockade'.

Towne] Marlowe translates the OPPIDUM of the old maps.

3 Duckets] The Venetian gold ducat was generally current in several countries.

6 *Padua*] Padua was famous for its ancient university, the 'nursery of arts' referred to in *The Taming of the Shrew*, I. i. 2.

8 liberall]] Both 'directed to intellectual enlargement and refinement' (*OED* 1), and the more common 'generous' (*OED* 2).

20 hooks] In *A Caveat for Common Cursetors* (London: W. Gryffyth, 1567), B4ᵛ–C1ʳ), Thomas Harman describes 'Hooker[s], or Angler[s]'—petty thieves who 'customably carry with them a staffe of v. or vi. foote long, in which within one ynch of the tope thereof is a little hole bored through in which hole they putte an yron hoke and with the same they wyll plucke vnto them quicly any thing that they may reche ther with".

25 Zoons] 'A euphemistic abbreviation of *by God's wounds* . . . used in oaths and asseverations' (*OED*).

28 by her attire] Bellamira probably appeared as the 'fair hot wench in flame-coloured taffeta' referred to in *1 Henry IV*, I. ii. 10.

Act III scene ii

3 It seems reasonable to attribute this line to Lodowicke rather than to Mathias. Clearly there has been some slight dislocation of the text (Bennett postulates a lost speech for Lodowick, Craik one for Mathias), and some confusion of the actions. At II. iii. 370–83, Barabas orders Ithimore to deliver a written challenge 'feign'd from *Lodowicke*', and says that he himself will go to Lodowick and 'feigne some lye' to incense the rivals. In III. iii. 20–2, Ithimore claims to have himself borne the challenging letters.

7 tall] brave.

10–19 These lines have something of the patterning of the classical 'lament', deriving from Greek tragedy and reaching an English pinnacle in *The Spanish Tragedy*. Cf. also *3 Henry VI*:

> These arms of mine shall be thy winding-sheet;
> My heart, sweet boy, shall be thy sepulchre.
>
> (II. v. 114–15.)

For a discussion of the 'lament' form, see Wolfgang Clemen, *English Tragedy before Shakespeare*, trans. T. S. Dorsch (London: Methuen, 1961), 211–86.

34 they reveal the] Dyce remarked that a verb has been omitted from Q ('they the'), and many editors accept his emendation to 'reveal'. Craik prefers Collier's suggested 'disclose' for its alliteration (dis*c*lose/*c*ausers).

Act III scene iii

3 held in hand] '(led) by the hand, or by a string' (*OED* 'hand', 29b).

10 bottle-nos'd knave] The dramatic convention of the Jew's nose extends before and beyond Barabas. In early drama the Jewish physiognomy was attributed to the devil (T. W. Craik, *The Tudor Interlude* (Leicester: University Press, 1958), 51). A later pamphlet, William Rowley's *A Search for Money* (1609), has a usurer whose 'visage (or vizard) [is] like the artificiall Jewe of Maltae's nose'.

22 *imprimis*] first of all; Ithimore is linguistically confused.

23 as the story sayes] A stock phrase of medieval narrative, which seems to demand the rhythmical correctness given by the inserted 'and'.

32 Fryars of St *Jaques*] The Dominican Black Friars, also known as Jacobins (cf. IV. i. 107), were so called from their first house in Paris, in the Rue St Jacques.

47 the Pryor] The reference must be to the Governor, the Grand Master of the Knights of St John, an apparently unprecedented and certainly erroneous usage; the title correctly designates the ruler of one of the priories into which the Order's eight Langues or Tongues were divided.

54 *Virgo, salve*] Greetings, maiden.

55 ducke] Abigall is perhaps curtseying to the Fryar.

67–8 My sinfull . . . misbeleefe] Marlowe seems to be drawing on a complex of sources for Abigall's summary of her spiritual dilemma. Dr Peter Fisher found a probable source for the 'Labyrinth' image in St Ambrose's commentary on Ps. 119 (118 in the numbering of the Vulgate), v. 59, with its description of the misguided souls who often run themselves into labyrinths of confusion, *erroris labyrinthos frequenter incurrunt* (*In Psalmum CXVIII expositio, sermo* 8. 31. 2, in Migne, *Patrologia latina*, xv. cols. 1306–7). Intermediary between the patristical origin of the image and Marlowe's usage may be a literary parallel (suggested to me by Professor Doug Bruster of the University of Chicago). The speaker in Poem XCV of Thomas Watson's *Hecatompathia* (1582) rejoices that she has at last 'found the way To leave the doubtfull Labyrinth of *Loue*' where she was enforced to stay 'till *Reason* taught [her] mind'; now she is resolved never again to 'leave the golden rule' of Reason, 'that stoode so much my friend'. The little scenario affords a comparable situation to that of Abigall, casting the Petrarchan Reason in the role of the Abbesse.

69 Sonne] the Son of God, i.e. Jesus Christ; cf. Rom. 6: 23, 'For the wages of sinne is death: but the gifte of God is eternall life through Iesus Christ our Lord'. Implicit in Marlowe's line is the usual pun on *son/sun*.

Act III scene iv

6 *Spurca*] the feminine form of Latin *spurcus* (= dirty, filthy), perhaps intended as an insult to Abigall.

15 second selfe] The repeated 'life' in Q was probably caught up from the previous line; the emendation allows Barabas to use the proper language of Classical friendship.

31 within my gates] Cf. Exod. 20: 10, Deut. 14: 21, etc.

33 *Cain* by *Adam*] In Genesis 4 Cain was cursed by God, not by Adam, for the murder of his brother.

42 servant . . . friend] The words of Barabas seem to parody those of Christ, 'Henceforthe, call I you not seruants: for the seruant knoweth not what his master doeth: but I have called you friends' (John 15: 15).

51 hold] bet, wager.

56 Well said] Well done (cf. C. T. Onions, *A Shakespeare Glossary*).

58 proverb] Tilley, S771.

66 messe of rice porredge] The chapter-heading for Genesis 25 in the Geneva Bible tells how Esau sold his birthright for a 'a messe of potage'. Marlowe returns to the word 'pottage' in l. 91.

71 Italian] Renaissance Italy was reputedly the home of the great poisoners.

Ancona] At the beginning of the sixteenth century the Adriatic port was the home of a thriving Jewish community; in 1556, however, Pope Paul IV ordered that all Ancona Jews should be either expelled, burned as heretics, or converted to Christianity (see Cecil Roth, *A History of the Marranos* (New York: Meridian Books, 1959), 205–8).

77 This Even they use] It is their custom on this night.

94 by the eye] *OED* 'eye' 4b, 'as much as you like'.

99 *Alexander*] Alexander the Great died (323 BC) of a fever, but one account of his death suggests that he was poisoned by one of his climbing followers; see Plutarch's *Life of Alexander*. A similar curse is pronounced in Ovid's *Ibis*, ll. 297–8:

> Nec tibi fida magis misceri pocula possint,
> Quam qui cornigero de Iove natus erat.

('May drinks be mixed for you that are no more dependable than the one prepared for the son [i.e. Alexander the Great] of horned Jupiter').

100 *Borgias*] It was popularly believed that Pope Alexander VI died after drinking poisoned wine which had been prepared—although intended for other victims—by his son, Cesare Borgia. Bawcutt suggests Sir Geoffrey Fenton, *The Historie of Guicciardin* (London: Thos. Vautiollier, 1579), 307–8, as a possible source for Marlowe's reference.

102 the blood . . . bane] After killing the Hydra, a water-snake which ravaged the town of Lerna, Hercules tipped his arrows with the poisonous blood. Cf. the 'winged snakes of *Lerna*' in the curse of Bajazeth (*1 Tamburlaine*, IV. iv. 21).

103 Hebon] Obviously a poison, although its exact nature is still unknown. Hamlet's father was poisoned (I. v. 62) with a concoction of 'hebona' (in the Quarto text), or 'hebenon' (Folio). The word derives from Latin *hebenus* (= ebony). The tree of '*Heben* sad' grew in Spenser's Garden of Proserpina (*Faerie Queene*, II. VII. 52) which was circled with 'a blacke flood which . . . is the river of *Cocytus* deepe'.

Cocitus] Cocytus was one of the rivers of Hades, which Virgil's priestess shows to Aeneas: *Cocyti stagna alta vides Stygiamque paludem* (*Aeneid*, vi. 323).

104 Stygian] Styx was the principal river of Hades.

114 Flanders mares] The allusion is clearly to the nuns, but its precise terms of reference are unclear. Henry VIII called Anne of Cleves 'a fat Flanders mare'. In Ford's *Love's Sacrifice* (1633) the phrase describes 'violently lascivious women' (Bawcutt): 'oh for three Barbary stone horses to top three Flanders mares' (III. i).

114–15 with a powder] *OED* 'impetuously, violently, in haste'; Tilley, P533.

Act III scene v

OSD BASSO] Q has plural 'Bashaws', but the addresses 'Great Sir' and 'Bashaw' in ll. 4 and 11 suggest that the singular is more appropriate.

5 Westerne *Inde*] The gold and silver mines of South America.

18 refluence] reflux.

30 Basiliskes] large cannon, probably made of brass.

35 more welcome is then warres] Cf. 'war to most men welcom', *Lucans First Booke*, 184.

Act III scene vi

OSD Q marks a double entry for Abigall here and after l. 6; a bookkeeper's hand may be suggested.

12 ghostly father] spiritual father, confessor.

18 desperate] In the theological sense, meaning 'without hope of salvation'; Abigall has learned that she will be damned if she does not confess her sins before she dies.

35 degraded] deprived of his holy orders; the Fryar exaggerates the penalty, however, when he includes burning at the stake.

42 exclaime on] accuse; a more emphatic form than 'exclaime against' at l. 46.

49 crucified a child] Anti-Jewish feeling in England gave rise to many completely unfounded stories of atrocities such as the kidnapping of young Christian children who were then crucified in mockery of Christ's crucifixion. Chaucer's Prioress tells a Tale about 'yonge Hugh of Lyncoln' who was 'slayn . . . With cursed Jewes'.

Act IV scene i

1 to] compared with.

21 *Cazzo*] Florio's dictionary, *A World of Words* (1598), glosses the Italian obscenity as 'a mans priuie member'. It is used as an expression of contempt in Marston's *Malcontent*, I. iii. 104 and V. iv. 26.

diabolo] the devil. Bawcutt retains Q's feminine form (= she-devil), and explains that it is 'directed at Abigail'.

23 Caterpillers] parasites; cf. *2 Henry VI*, IV. iv. 37–8: 'All scholars, lawyers, courtiers, gentlemen, They call false caterpillars'.

50 inmates] Barabas ingratiates himself with the Fryars, implying that they now share all his secrets. Craik follows Broughton in reading 'inmate' and making this part of the aside to Ithimore.

57 A hundred for a hundred] interest of 100% on a loan.

60 lost] damned.

65 on my knees . . . *Jerusalem*] To make a pilgrimage to a holy place was a regular Christian act of penitence; and it is still not unusual for pilgrims to complete part of the journey on their knees. Barabas, of course, exaggerates the distance he is prepared thus to travel.

66 Sollers] solars, lofts or attics used for storage.

74–5 *Florence . . . Mosco*] Barabas lists the important financial centres of the sixteenth century.

77 bancho] *OED* cites this line to illustrate the Italian form of the word (= bank).

87 Q assigns this line to 1 Fryar, but I agree with Bawcutt that it makes dramatic sense for 2 Fryar to counter the charge in l. 85 that 'their laws are strict'; this also gives evidence for Barabas's comment in l. 107 that 2 Fryar (Bernardine) has 'Malign'd the order of the Jacobines'. It could be argued, however, that 'they goe bare-foot too' more properly describes one of the orders of 'discalced' (shoeless) friars such as the Franciscans.

98 thee rogue] Q's 'thee goe' fails to supply the insult that 1 Fryar's retort needs.

103–4 Q assigns the first of these lines to '*Ith.*', omitting any prefix for the second. The present assignment allows Barabas to speak *both* to the Fryar—reassuring Bernardine of his favour—*and* (conspiratorially) to Ithimore.

107 the order of the Jacobines] See III. iii. 30 n.

113 shriv'd] confessed (Barabas must confess his sins before he is baptized).

117 So now] 'Barabas's soliloquy marks a suspension of dramatic time' (Craik); it is now much later in the evening.

124 requisite he should not] Q places the 'not' before 'requisite', implying a stress *requisite* otherwise unknown in Marlowe, who uses *réquisite* at II. ii. 239 above and also at *1 Tamburlaine*, III. i. 47, *2 Tamburlaine*, I. i. 50, III. i. 71, and *Dr Faustus*. I. i. 156. The transposition was suggested by Deighton (see on I. iii. 22), 121–2.

131 so] Barabas makes a gesture—perhaps of slitting the throat—to indicate his intention.

137 order] The rules of their Order would not permit the friars to undress completely at night, only to lie down in their habits.

143 shake his heeles] The phrase is usually used to describe death by hanging.

146 strangle] Cf. the strangling of the Cardinal in *The Massacre at Paris*, scene xviii.

147 use to confesse] practise the making and hearing of confessions.

148 proverb] Barabas quotes a very common proverb (Tilley, C587).

162 proceed] *OED* gives this as the earliest example of *proceed* 3e, 'To make progress, advance; to prosper'.

185 his] The genitive form of 'it'.

192 staid] were late.

205 the staffe] Murder weapons (or their value) were forfeit to the authorities.

Act IV scene ii

7–8 man of another world] ghost or spirit.

11 tall] fine.

16 *Non-plus*] state of bewilderment.

critical aspect] forbidding appearance; 'aspect' has something of its astrological sense (*OED* 4).

19 free-hold] property, 'patch'.

20 neck-verse] The ability to read, in Latin, the first verse of Ps. 51 entitled a criminal to plead 'benefit of clergy' and escape the gallows.

22 hempen] The hangman's noose was made of hemp, and the adjective was extended to describe all associated matters, cf. 'hempen tippet' at l. 28.

Hodie tibi, cras mihi] The proverb—meaning 'your turn today, mine tomorrow'—was common in Latin and in English: Tilley, T371.

24 Exercise] act of devotion, i.e. the ceremony of the execution.

28 Tippet] stole, especially one worn by a priest.

30 Cure] parish (cure of souls).

32 muschatoes] moustache.

46 Turke of ten pence] worthless fellow; *OED* suggests that the phrase is original with Marlowe.

51 family] *OED* 1, 'The servants of a house or establishment; the household'; cf. also sense 8, 'The thieving fraternity'.

51–2 stand or fall] The sexual implications are obvious—and may link the 'family' with the Family of Love, a puritan sect whose name gave rise to easy innuendoes.

55 cleane] Two senses of *clean* (= 'completely' *and* = 'not dirty') allow Ithimore to make his pun.

63 *Allamira*] Perhaps, as Craik suggests, a mispronunciation of 'Bellamira'; Bawcutt sees, and corrects, a printer's error.

67 Partridges] Pliny, *Natural History*, x. 100, records the habits of partridges: 'they cover their egges with a soft carpet or hilling as it were of fine dust: neither doe they sit where they laid them first, nor yet in a place which they suspect to bee much frequented with resort of passengers, but convey them to some other place' (trans. Philemon Holland (London, 1601), 289, cit. Bawcutt).

91 in his kinde] according to his nature, i.e. as he deserves; but 'to use someone like a Jew' proverbially described harsh ill-treatment (Tilley, J52).

93 lye in my lap] cf. IV. iv. 30; the obscene implications of the phrase are explored in *Hamlet*:

Ham. Lady, shall I lie in your lap?
Oph. No, my lord.
Ham. I mean, my head upon your lap?
Oph. Ay, my lord.
Ham. Do you think I meant country matters?   (III. ii. 112–16)

94 running Banquet . . . rags] Bellamira now imitates the Queen in Marlowe's *Dido Queene of Carthage* (Act II scene i), where Dido entertains Aeneas at her banquet and expresses horror at his 'base robes'.

99–109] On these lines, Michel Poirier comments: 'In Marlowe's works, allusions to pastoral Greece linked with the theme of invitation have given rise to several gems of pure poetry sparkling here and there. One of them has been inserted beyond all probability into the part of the villainous slave' (*Christopher Marlowe* (London, 1951), 162).

101 *Jason* . . . Fleece] Jason was the 'vent'rous youth of Greece' (*Hero and Leander*, l. 56) who sailed to Colchis with the Argonauts to recover the golden fleece. The fleece was that of the ram which carried Phrixus and Helle when they escaped from Thebes. Cf. Bassanio's description of Portia in *Merchant of Venice*:

> her sunny locks
> Hang on her temples like a golden fleece,
> Which makes her seat of Belmont Colchis' strond,
> And many Jasons come in quest of her.
> (I. i. 169–72.)

102 painted Carpets] i.e. brightly coloured flowers.

105 *Adonis* . . . Loves Queene] The passion of Venus, goddess of love, for the beautiful Adonis is one of the most popular legends of classical mythology.

108 *Dis*] The classical god of the underworld.

109 Shalt . . . love] Ithimore seems to parody Marlowe's own lyric poem 'Come live with mee, and be my love'; cf. *Works*, 214–15.

113 give down] 'Of a cow: to let flow (milk)', *OED*.

124 'parrell] apparel.

126–7 gray groat] silver coin of little value.

127 Reame] Ithimore puns on 'ream' (= quantity of paper) and 'realm' (= kingdom).

141 runs division] a musical term for the division of long notes into many short ones.

145 ten thousand nights] Ithimore is still in his exaggerated heroic mode. Jove made three nights into one when he lay with Alcmena and sired Hercules.

Act IV scene iii

3 wont] accustomed.

5 *Coupe de Gorge*] I'll cut his throat.

6 totter'd] tattered; both forms are common in Elizabethan English.

8 winds . . . eare] The gesture is similar to that performed by a comparable villain in *Arden of Faversham*: 'His chin was bare, but on his upper lip A mutchado, which he wound about his ear' (iii. 51–2). In his edition of that play (London: Methuen, 1973), M. L. Wine suggests that this may have been a stock description of such a character.

12 Catzerie] *OED* derives this word from *cazzo* (cf. IV. i. 21 n.) and suggests 'cheating, trickery'; there are no other examples.

13 crosbiting] swindling, outwitting.

14 husband . . . whores] possibly a pimp, who lives on the earnings of his 'wives'.

19 wantst . . . tale] is anything lacking from the amount you should have?

51 as unknowne] i.e. as yet unknown to Barabas.

63 demand] Most editors agree that a word has dropped out at this place.

Act IV scene iv

6SD CURTEZANE] Q assigns this line to '*Pilia*', but sense suggests that it is Bellamira who speaks, urging Ithimore to honour his toast— and hoping to make him drunk.

12 *Rivo Castiliano*] The Italian phrase, which could only mean 'river of Castile', seems to be an expression of drunken delight; cf. *Henry IV Pt 1*, 'Rivo! says the drunkard' (II. iv. 107).

24 snicle . . . fast] The phrase has never been satisfactorily explained, but it clearly indicates complicity.

27 for me] as far as I am concerned.

31 Love . . . long] The phrase was proverbial; it is used by Christmas (l. 1697) in *Summers Last Will and Testament* (1600), and McKerrow observes that 'Hazlitt notes that this occurs in Heywood's *Epigrams* (1562). It is also in his *Proverbs*, ed. Sharman, p. 98' (*The Works of Thomas Nashe*, ed. R. B. McKerrow, corrected by F. P. Wilson (Oxford: Basil Blackwell, 1966), vol. iv. 441). But Ithimore could also be singing (and calling for a musician to 'rumble' in continuation) a snatch of a popular ballad, perhaps that recorded by H. E. Rollins in 'An Analytical Index to the ballad entries (1557–1709) in The Register of the Company of Stationers of London' (*Studies in Philology*, 21 (1924), no. 1). Robert Lindsey has found such a lyric reprinted in an anthology, *Corn from Olde Fields*, ed. Eleanor H.

Brougham (London: John Lane, 1918), 140, although its prove-
nance—'a Manuscript of about 1610'—is vague.

31–2 let . . . tumble] Bennett compares the description in *The Two
Italian Gentlemen* (1585) of 'these fine Criminadoes, that can tumble
in a Gentlewomans lap, and rumble in her eare' (sig. G4).

32 incony] fine, delicate; cf. also Marlowe, *Ovids Elegies*, I. x. 21–2:

> The whore stands to be bought for each mans mony
> And seekes vild wealth by selling of her Cony.

34 tuna] Lake notes similarities between the language here and that
in plays by Thomas Dekker such as *Old Fortunatus*.

37 Gramercy] thank you.

47 poyson'd] Cf. *Edward II*, 'I learn'd in Naples how to poison
flowers' (v. iv. 31).

48 cats guts] i.e. the lute strings.

49 chitterlins] chitterlings, black puddings: 'smaller intestines of
beasts, as of the pig, *esp.* as an article of food prepared by frying or boil-
ing', *OED*.

55 fingers] plays on the lute skilfully.

57 runnes] plays a rapid sequence of notes.

74 *Judas*] Judas Iscariot, the Apostle who betrayed Christ. His sui-
cide is recorded in the Gospels (e.g. Matt. 27: 3–5), but the belief
that 'Judas was hang'd on an Elder' (*Love's Labour's Lost*, v. v. 601) is
medieval. The hat seems to be Marlowe's addition.

76 *Cham*] 'an obsolete form of Khan formerly commonly applied to
the rulers of the Tartars and Mongols, and to the Emperor of China',
OED.

77 masty] *OED*, 'of a swine: fattened'; Craik reads 'nasty', and
Bawcutt has 'musty'.

Act V scene i

5 Towne . . . wals] Marlowe is inventing a battle in which the
Turks, a sea-borne force, attack the walled inland city of Mdina
(marked as 'Oppidum' on sixteenth century maps of Malta).

40 bondman] Bennett explains that in medieval law a slave could
not testify against his master.

43 I'le live] In Dyce's emendation (Q 'I live'), Barabas asserts his
determination to go on living, despite his enemies' ill-will.

57 the heavens are just] cf. Wisd. 11: 13 (Vulgate 11: 17): 'that
wherewith a man sinneth, by the same also shal he be punished'; also

King Lear, v. iii. 171–2: 'The gods are just, and of our pleasant vices
Make instruments to plague us.'

60 throw that o're the wals] Craik offers an attractive explanation
for the action that ensues: 'probably the body was simply tossed forward and allowed to roll towards the front of the platform (the
Governor's "So" certainly suggests that his command has been exe-
cuted to his satisfaction). It would then lie for a moment in full view,
an object of anticipatory interest, until Barabas's rising.'

66–7 to slay ... downe] The threat is almost formulaic with
Marlowe; cf. *Dr Faustus*, v. 278–80; *Edward II*, I. iv. 100–2, *Massacre
at Paris*, xxii. 1201–2.

82 Poppy and cold mandrake juyce] The most powerful opiates
known to Elizabethan dramatists; cf. *Othello*, III. iii. 330.

87 make *Malta* ours] This episode seems to be referred to by John
Webster in *The Devil's Law-case* (*c.*1617; ed. E. M. Brennan, London:
Ernest Benn, Ltd., 1975) where Romelio promises to 'be a rare
Italianated Jew ... [and] Betray a town to th'Turk' (III. ii. 1–16).

88 Sluice] Broughton: a barrier regulating water-flow. Dyce emends
to 'Trench', but Van Fossen retains Q's 'Truce', explaining 'against
the truce' as 'either (1) contrary to the treaty or (2) in anticipation of
the cessation of hostilities'.

91 channels] sewers.

99 doom'd] sentenced.

Act V scene ii

1 vaile] lower [a ship's sails] in token of submission; the literal use
of the word is found in II. ii. 11.

3 Now where's ... haughty *Spaine*] A natural sentiment for
Englishmen in the years after the Armada, but also hinting at the
criticisms made of the Spanish viceroy of Sicily, Don Garcia de
Toledo, for delay in relieving the historical siege; in his defence see
H. J. A. Sire, *The Knights of Malta* (New Haven and London: Yale
University Press, 1994), 71 n.

16 Janizaries] The *corps d'élite* of the Turkish infantry, usually
employed to guard the sultan.

24 Captives] Q Captaines; the same emendation is called for in
Lucans First Booke, l. 510.

40 the Asse that *Aesope* speaketh of] The ass is shown in Geoffrey
Whitney, *Choice of Emblemes* (Leiden: Plantin, 1586), where it denotes

the rich man who does not enjoy his wealth; cf. also Tilley, A360. There is no source in Aesop for the emblem.

44 Occasion] The *Disticha Catonis* taught the medieval and Renaissance schoolboy that 'Fronte capillata, post est Occasio calva' (II. xxvi. 2). Hence in Renaissance iconography, Occasion (or Opportunity) is personified as a naked female with a long forelock which must be seized immediately: she is bald behind. Cf. Erwin Panofsky, *Studies in Iconology* (New York: Harper and Row, 1972), 72.

79 out-house] A building outside the city walls, cf. v. iii. 37. This sense is not recorded in *OED*.

Act V scene iii

3 Two lofty Turrets. . . . Towne] In Q, which is followed by Bowers, this line is set *after* the present l. 10 ('And . . . *Sicily*'). Craik argues convincingly that the phrase 'Two lofty Turrets' stands in apposition to 'ruines', but he (followed by Bawcutt) repositions the line after l. 5 ('We . . . entry'). The present position makes 'Turrets' the immediate referent for 'Which' in line 4. On old maps, twin forts—St Angelo and St Elmo—are marked with turrets at the entrance to Malta's main harbour. St Elmo was in fact captured by the Turks in the Great Siege.

9 contermur'd] Q contermin'd: (see I. iii. 22 n).

other petty Iles] i.e. Gozo, Comino, Cominotto.

11 *Siracusian Dionisius*] Dionysius the Elder (405–367/6 BC).

Act V scene iv

3 Culverin] a kind of cannon, with a long muzzle.

4 Linstocke] a staff about one metre long with a forked head to hold a lighted match which was used to ignite cannon.

Act V scene v

6 Sacke] Spanish white wine.

9 and dye] Barabas has probably poisoned the contents of his wine-cellars.

27 field-pieces] light cannon for use on the battlefield.

39 warning-peece] a gun fired as a signal or alarm.

49 worldlings] Barabas addresses the audience directly, assuming that they will share his attachment to worldly matters.

49 underneath the sunne] Cf. Eccles. 1: 3, 9 'under the sunne'.

88 curse . . . dye] Barabas follows the advice given by Job's wife, who told her husband to 'Blaspheme God, and dye' (Job 2: 9).

Epistle

Thomas Heywood dedicated two of his own plays, Part II of *The Fair Maid of the West* (1631) and Part I of *The Iron Age* (1632) to Thomas Hammon, a barrister who was admitted to Gray's Inn in 1611.

3 *Allin*] The actor Edward Alleyn, 1566–1626.

4 usher'd] announced, introduced.

Court] The title page claims that the play was presented before the King and Queen 'in his Majesties Theatre at *White-Hall*'—which was perhaps the Cockpit-in-Court, remodelled as a theatre in 1629–30; cf. G. E. Bentley, *The Jacobean and Caroline Stage* (Oxford: Clarendon Press, 1941–68), vi. 259–84.

5 Cock-pit] The Phoenix or Cockpit theatre in Drury Lane was one of the two principal Caroline playhouses; cf. ibid. 47.

6 newly] The word could mean either 'recently, for the first time', or else 'afresh, for the second time'.

16 New-yeares gift] Gifts were exchanged at New Year rather than at Christmas.

Prologue to the Stage

6 A lasting memorie] Heywood seems to think that the narrative poem *Hero and Leander* gave more prestige to Marlowe than his plays.

10 *Proteus*] a sea-god who had the power to change his shape, described by Homer in book iv of the *Odyssey*.

Roscius] The most famous of Roman actors, *d.* by 62 BC.

12 *Perkins*] Richard Perkins, a leading actor who died 1650.

(Second) Epilogue

1 *Pigmalion*] Pygmalion, the legendary King of Cyprus who fell in love with his own handiwork, the statue of a beautiful woman.

2 *Apelles*] A famous Greek painter of the 4th century BC.

SELECT BIBLIOGRAPHY

Editions of The Jew of Malta *since 1900*

1. *In Collected Works*

BENNETT, H. S. (ed.), *The Jew of Malta* and *The Massacre at Paris* in *The Works and Life of Christopher Marlowe*, ed. R. H. Case (London: Methuen, 1930–3), iii (1931).

BOWERS, FREDSON (ed.), *The Complete Works of Christopher Marlowe* (2 vols., London: Cambridge University Press, 1973), i.

GILL, ROMA (ed.), *The Plays of Christopher Marlowe* (London: Oxford University Press, 1971).

KIRSCHBAUM, LEO (ed.), *The Plays of Christopher Marlowe* (Cleveland and New York: World Publishing Company (Meridian Books), 1962).

PENDRY, E. D., and MAXWELL, J. C. (eds.), *Christopher Marlowe: Complete Plays and Poems* (London: Dent; Totowa, NJ: Bowman and Littlefield, 1976).

TUCKER BROOKE, C. F. (ed.), *The Works of Christopher Marlowe* (Oxford: Clarendon Press, 1910).

2. *Single Text Editions*

The Famous Tragedy of The Rich Jew of Malta: A Scolar Press Facsimile (Menston: Scolar Press, 1970).

BAWCUTT, N. W. (ed.), *The Jew of Malta* (London: Manchester University Press; Baltimore: Johns Hopkins University Press, 1978).

CRAIK, T. W. (ed.), *The Jew of Malta* (London: Ernest Benn Ltd., 1966).

VAN FOSSEN, R. W. (ed.), *The Jew of Malta* (Regent's Renaissance Drama Series; London: Edward Arnold; Lincoln, Nebr.: University of Nebraska Press, 1964).

Critical Studies

1. *General Studies of Marlowe and his Works*

BAKELESS, J., *The Tragicall History of Christopher Marlowe* (Cambridge, Mass.: Harvard University Press, 1942).

BEVINGTON, D. M., *From 'Mankind' to Marlowe* (Cambridge, Mass.: Harvard University Press, 1962).

BOAS, F. S. *Christopher Marlowe* (Oxford: Clarendon Press, 1940).

BRADBROOK, M. C., *Themes and Conventions of Elizabethan Tragedy* (London: Cambridge University Press, 1935; 2nd edn. 1952).

COLE, D., *Suffering and Evil in the Plays of Christopher Marlowe* (Princeton University Press, 1962).

ELIOT, T. S., 'Christopher Marlowe', in *Selected Essays* (London: Faber & Faber, 1932, 3rd edn. 1961; repr. Clifford Leech (ed.), *Marlowe: A Collection of Critical Essays*: Englewood Cliffs, NJ: Prentice-Hall, Inc., 1964).

ELLIS-FERMOR, U. M., *Christopher Marlowe* (London: Methuen, 1927).

FRIEDENREICH, K., GILL, R., and KURIYAMA, C. B. (eds.), *A Poet and a Filthy Play-Maker: Essays on Christopher Marlowe* (New York: AMS Press, 1988).

HENDERSON, P., *Marlowe* (London: Longmans, Green & Co., 1952).

KOCHER, P. H., *Christopher Marlowe* (Chapel Hill: University of North Carolina Press, 1946).

LEECH, C., *Christopher Marlowe: Poet for the Stage* (New York: AMS Press, 1986).

LEVIN, H., *The Overreacher* (London: Faber & Faber, 1952).

MAXWELL, J. C., "The Plays of Christopher Marlowe', in B. Ford (ed.), *A Guide to English Literature, II: The Age of Shakespeare* (London: Pelican Books, 1955).

NICHOLL, C., *The Reckoning* (London: Jonathan Cape, 1992).

POIRIER, M., *Christopher Marlowe* (London: Chatto & Windus, 1951).

STEANE, J. B., *Marlowe* (Cambridge University Press, 1964).

WILSON, F. P., *Marlowe and the Early Shakespeare* (Oxford: Clarendon Press, 1953).

2. *Particular Studies of* The Jew of Malta

BABB, H. S., 'Policy in Marlowe's *The Jew of Malta*, *English Literary History*, 24 (1957), 85–94.

BAWCUTT, N. W., 'Machiavelli and Marlowe's *The Jew of Malta*', *Renaissance Drama*, NS 3 (1970), 3–49.

CARTELLI, T., 'Endless Play: The False Starts of Marlowe's *Jew of Malta*' in Friedenreich *et al.*, 117–28.

DEATS, S., 'Biblical Parody in Marlowe's *The Jew of Malta*: A Re-examination', *Christianity and Literature*, 27/2 (Winter, 1988), 27–47.

—— and STARKS, S. L., ' "So neatly plotted, and so well perform'd": Villain as Playwright in Marlowe's *The Jew of Malta*', *Theatre Journal*, 44 (1992), 375–89.

DESSEN, A. C., 'The Elizabethan Stage Jew and Christian Example: Gerontus, Barabas and Shylock', *Modern Language Quarterly*, 35 (1974), 231–45.

HARBAGE, A., 'Innocent Barabas', *Tulane Drama Review*, 8 (1964), 47–58.

HUNTER, G. K., 'The Theology of Marlowe's *The Jew of Malta*', *Journal of the Warburg and Courtauld Institutes*, 27 (1964), 211–40; repr. in id., *Dramatic Identities and Cultural Tradition: Studies in Shakespeare and his Contemporaries* (Liverpool: University Press, 1978), 60–102.

RIBNER, I., 'Marlowe and Machiavelli', *Comparative Literature*, 6 (1954), 349–50.

ROCKLIN, E. L., 'Marlowe as Experimental Dramatist: The Role of the Audience in *The Jew of Malta*', in Friedenreich *et al.*, 129–42.

SIMMONS, J. L., 'Elizabethan Stage Practice and Marlowe's *The Jew of Malta*', *Renaissance Drama*, NS 4 (1971), 93–104.

SMITH, J. L., '*The Jew of Malta* in the Theatre', in Brian Morris (ed.), *Christopher Marlowe* (Mermaid Critical Commentaries; London, 1968).